GOD IS
HERE

GOD IS HERE

Reimagining
the Divine

TOBA SPITZER

ST. MARTIN'S
ESSENTIALS
NEW YORK

First published in the United States by St. Martin's Essentials, an imprint of St. Martin's Publishing Group

www.stmartins.com

Library of Congress Cataloging-in-Publication Data

Names: Spitzer, Toba, author.
Title: God is here : reimagining the Divine / Toba Spitzer.
Description: First edition. | New York : St. Martin's Essentials, 2022. | Includes bibliographical references.
Identifiers: LCCN 2021046524 | ISBN 9781250764492 (hardcover) | ISBN 9781250764508 (ebook)
Subjects: LCSH: God (Judaism)—Philosophy. | Bible. Old Testament—Criticism, interpretation, etc.
Classification: LCC BM610 .S64 2022 | DDC 296.3/11—dc23
LC record available at https://lccn.loc.gov/2021046524

Our books may be purchased in bulk for promotional, educational, or business use. Please contact your local bookseller or the Macmillan Corporate and Premium Sales Department at 1-800-221-7945, extension 5442, or by email at MacmillanSpecia!Markets@macmillan.com.

First Edition: 2022

10   9   8   7   6   5   4   3   2   1

To my father, for his love of Water, and to my mother,
for her gift of Voice

In memory of Gina M. Fried, Rock of my heart

CONTENTS

· · · · · · · · · ·

INTRODUCTION

. . . .

L et's say you walk into a restaurant that you've heard a lot about. You're looking for something to satisfy your hunger and give you strength to get through the day. The waiter hands you the menu, and you sit back, scanning all the sections—salads, soups, lunch, dinner. You begin to realize, sadly, that nothing on the menu looks particularly appetizing. The choices sound bland, unsatisfying, or just strange. Much of the menu is incomprehensible. Resigned, or maybe even a little bit angry, you put the menu down and leave. You convince yourself that you're not so hungry after all and head into your day.

This is what happens to many of us as we realize we have a spiritual hunger. The body needs food to survive, and, while it may not hit us in as obvious a way, our spirits also need to be fed. Yet, so often, we either don't know where to go to satisfy this hunger, or the places we do know about just don't satisfy. We walk into the "restaurant" of organized religion and realize there's just too much we can't swallow.

We all need a system of meaning to make sense of our lives, to help us answer big questions. Why am I here on this earth? What should I be doing to make a difference in the world? How do I instill values that are important to me in my children? What are the right choices to make—about work, about what to do with the money I have, about complicated ethical situations? How do I make sense of difficult events in my life, loss, and sorrow? In confusing and challenging times, what can I do to bring calm, clarity, and joy into my day-to-day living?

Religions of every sort came into existence to help answer these questions. Because every religion came into being in a specific time and place, and were created by specific groups of people, there are differences in how each one answers universal questions about life and death, meaning and morals. What all religions share is an awareness of Something both within and beyond us, a Power that shapes and guides our lives, especially if we actively seek It out.

For those of us raised in the Jewish, Christian, and Muslim religions, that Power is called, in English, God. While the stories about God, and what it means to serve God, differ greatly in the Abrahamic religions, there is a cluster of ideas that, for most people, define what God is: very big and awesome, holding ultimate power over us, a force for ultimate good. And even though the religions differ greatly on how explicit we can be about God's humanlike qualities, most people who talk about God use very human language to describe what God does and is. God knows, God acts, God loves, God judges, God gives and takes away life. No one would use those verbs to describe a river, or an electrical current, or a hurricane. So somewhere in the back of our minds, whether we explicitly believe it or not, God is a Big Person who knows everything and can do anything God wants.

The problem is, many of us just can't believe in a God like that. We can't, we just *won't*, believe in a Big Person that controls the world and our own lives like a puppet master. We know that we can turn to science to explain what happens in the natural world. Our own experience tells us that we have free will, that our choices are real. We can't believe in Someone or Something that we're told is both all-powerful and all-good, because when we look around the world, when we look at our own lives, it's very clear that there's a whole lot of not-good there. So either God is irrelevant, or not so good, or just not very plausible.

So we fold up the menu and push back from the table. God doesn't exist, and religion is either obsolete or a force for bad. We take our spiritual hunger somewhere else, where a God-belief isn't required (meditation, perhaps, or a yoga class), or we try to ignore our spiritual hunger by going shopping, or watching TV, or preoccupying ourselves with work or alcohol or sex.

This book is my attempt to create a new menu, because I believe the hunger is real for most people, even those who say they have no interest in religion or God. I believe we all need spiritual practices to ground us, to make us stronger and more compassionate. I believe religious communities can be models for creating the kind of society we want to inhabit: communities where we can live values of justice and love, and teach our children to be good and caring people. I believe that all human beings need meaningful rituals to mark important life transitions—whether welcoming a child into our lives, beginning and ending intimate relationships, mourning the deaths of those we love, or preparing for our own deaths.

And perhaps most importantly, I believe that we need to have language to talk about Something that is greater than ourselves, and greater than the things that our consumer culture tells us are ultimate. We need to believe in *something,* and the fact is we all do believe in something. So the question isn't really: Should I believe? But rather: What do I believe *in*? What do I think has ultimate value? To whom, and how, am I connected, beyond the tiny circle of my family? What are my responsibilities—to myself, to the people around me, to my society, to the planet? And what is there, beyond myself, that supports and sustains those values, connections, and commitments?

At a time when the human race is confronting the enormity of our destructive power in the context of climate change, we need to reject two myths. First, that a superhero God is going to magically appear and save us. And second, that human beings are so good and so powerful we can save ourselves. In between those two misconceptions is a deeper, urgent truth: there is Something operating both within us and around us that, if understood and accessed properly, can help us foster the wisdom, compassion, and resilience to perhaps save ourselves and our planet. We need to know It by Its many names, and learn from each of those names what is asked of us. This book is a step toward doing just that.

1

· · · · ·

METAPHORICALLY SPEAKING

What Metaphor Is and Why It's Important

When I read books by people who believe in God, and by those who don't, I've noticed that they share one basic assumption: that when we're talking about "God," we're referring to some kind of superpower entity, a Someone or a Something "out there" that exerts Its influence over us. Theologians of all different stripes try to make sense of this entity, how It works and how best to understand Him (or sometimes Her/Them). Atheists and humanists reject the whole idea of God because, they assert, there is nothing "out there" beyond what can be explained by the natural sciences and human nature. The crux of the debate between God-believers and God-nonbelievers is whether there is any truth to God's existence.

I'd like to suggest an entirely different way of thinking about the issue. What if, instead of arguing about whether or not God exists, or trying to come up with a definition of "God" that will finally convince everyone, we took a look at *us*? I invite you to accompany me into the realm of cognitive linguistics, the first step in creating our new "menu" of ways of thinking about, and experiencing, God.

Based on the work of George Lakoff, Mark Johnson, and others who seek to understand how human beings make meaning of the world around us, it is crucial to understand the central role of *metaphor*. "Metaphor" in this understanding isn't just a literary turn of phrase, like "Her eyes were deep pools of mystery." Rather, metaphors provide the framework for how we understand and talk about much of what makes us human.

For example, we tend to associate happiness and other positive feelings with the physical sensation of being "up," while "down" is associated with sad feelings. We say, "I'm feeling *up* today" or "I'm *high* on life" when we're in a good mood, and "I'm feeling so *low*" or "That really brought me *down*" when we're not. Why? As the writer James Geary explains, "Because we are literally up (i.e., vertical) when we are active, alert, and awake and we are literally down (i.e., horizontal) when we are sluggish, sleepy, or sick."[1] This association of "up" with positive and powerful and "down" with sad and weak is so fundamental that we may not even realize that we're using a metaphor to describe our feelings.

In this understanding, our minds use metaphors to translate our concrete, embodied experiences to things we experience that are very real but are not physical—like ideas, or arguments, or love. For example, most people would agree that love exists. We've experienced it in many ways—as a child or a parent, as a friend or a spouse, as a pet owner or a student. Yet we know that love is not a "thing," not something we can point to and say, "There it is!" While there are physical aspects of love—those things that happen in our brains and in our bodies when we experience different sorts of love—most of us wouldn't say that these neurological and chemical reactions equal "love."

So if love is more than a bodily process, what is it? When we think about love, and when we talk about it, we use what are called *conceptual metaphors,* drawing from other areas of our lives to make sense of our experiences of love. Lakoff and Johnson, in their research, have found these common metaphors for love:

LOVE IS A PHYSICAL FORCE: "I could feel the *electricity* between us"; "She's very *attracted* to him." LOVE IS MADNESS: "I'm *crazy* about them"; "She constantly *raves* about her." LOVE IS WAR: "He *fled* from their advances";

"She *won* her heart." And there are many more: Love as a Journey, as a Patient, as Magic.[2] Usually, we make use of these conceptual metaphors in a relatively unconscious way. We don't think, *Now I'm going to describe love as a kind of madness,* before we say, "He's *crazy* about her."

Another very basic conceptual metaphor in our culture is IDEAS ARE FOOD. We may not realize it, but we function within this metaphor all the time—whenever we "chew over" a suggestion, or wonder whether we can "digest" a particularly shocking idea, or marvel over how our child "devours" a new book. One of my favorite metaphors is ANGER IS A HOT LIQUID IN A CONTAINER, expressed in phrases like "I'm steamed up," or "She's boiling mad," or "He blew his top."

In many cultures today, a powerful metaphor is TIME IS A LIMITED RESOURCE or TIME IS MONEY. We *spend* time, we *lose* time, we *budget* our time. And we don't just talk about time this way, we actually *experience* it this way, as anyone who has "wasted" an afternoon in a doctor's waiting room or felt good about "spending" their time wisely knows.

But not everyone in the world experiences time like this; in fact, most people didn't until the past few hundred years, when industrialization introduced the idea that people get paid based on how many hours they work. It is quite possible to experience time in other ways—for example, as an endless flow. If time is not experienced through the metaphor of being a precious and limited resource, then waiting hours for a bus or a doctor's appointment doesn't feel like a "waste of time." While "time" is certainly something real, how we understand it and experience it depends on the unconscious metaphors within which we function.

In recent decades, cognitive scientists have been able to see how metaphorical reasoning functions in our brains. There are areas of our brains that are active not just when we are doing an action but also when we are just *thinking metaphorically* about doing that action. For example, when I contemplate "kicking a habit," the part of my brain that is involved when I physically kick something is activated, making the metaphor "real" in a powerful way. In another example, our early experience as infants being held by an adult and feeling their physical warmth becomes connected, via neurons, to our emotional understanding of affection. We express this metaphorically when we say things like "My friend is a very warm person." The metaphor AFFECTION IS WARMTH is much more than a turn of phrase—it becomes a basic way that we experience personal interactions.

Lakoff and Johnson write:

In all aspects of life . . . we define our reality in terms of metaphors and then proceed to act on the basis of the metaphors. We draw inferences, set goals, make commitments, and execute plans, all on the basis of how we in part structure our experience, consciously and unconsciously, by means of metaphor.[3]

The "metaphors we live by" are central to who we are, how we act, and how we make meaning of the world around us.

Metaphor and the "Real World"

Why do I think all of this is important? Because this new science of the brain tells us something intriguing about what "truth" is, which leads us back to the discussion about whether or not God exists. One of our most basic assumptions about the world is that there is a reality "out there," and that all that our senses and our brains are doing is telling us (more or less clearly, depending on the quality of our senses and our brains) what that reality *is*.

But if we accept that our minds use metaphors to make sense of large parts of our experience, then we need to shift a bit in how we think about what's "true." This means that even in the realm of science, where we tend to believe that we are getting at what's "really" going on in the world, things are a little more complicated. As the scientist and author Theodore Brown observes in his exploration of the role of conceptual metaphor in the work of science: "In this way of looking at things, truth is the product of human reasoning. It follows that science does not proceed by discovering preexisting truths about the world. Rather, it consists in observing the world and formulating truths about it."[4]

This statement doesn't mean that there is no reality, or that we can't make true and untrue statements. What it does mean is that truth—at least, the truth as far as we can know it—arises from an interaction of our bodies and brains and the world around us. What is "true" for us is some combination of what's actually going on in the world, and our experience of it. Because of this interaction, what we know as "true" can change and develop as we learn new things about the world and as we create new metaphors for understanding it. This is how we can go from thinking that the sun literally "rises" above the horizon to describing how planets move around the sun, or how the study of physics can evolve from Newton's theory of gravity to Einstein's theory of relativity. Instead of embodying some abstract, ultimate "truth," different ideas and theories help us make sense of the world around us, and help us live in that world. A good theory will explain things well and give us tools to live in ways that are productive. At the same time, it might be replaced at any time by a new theory that brings us a new understanding of "truth" and that gives us new and different abilities and awareness.

I imagine it's hard for most of us to accept the notion that how we know things is limited by the way our minds and bodies work. We're used to thinking that there's a world "out there" that we can make sense of "in here" in our minds; that when we talk about the sky being blue, the sky is blue. But color is not an inherent quality of the things around us; it is something we perceive based on the interplay of our eyes, our brains, and the way light reflects off objects we're looking at. Does this mean color is not "real"? Of course not. Color is an essential aspect of human experience and the universe around us. So on the one hand—as far as our daily lives are concerned—"The sky is blue" is a true statement, even if we can show scientifically that the quality "blue" is not inherently part of our atmosphere.

Coming back to the notion that science "consists in observing the world and formulating truths about it," rather than "discovering preexisting truths," I would argue that if this is true for the sciences, how much more so for religion!

Based on new understandings of how our minds work, we can borrow Theodore Brown's insight and say that "*religion* does not proceed by discovering preexisting truths about the world. Rather, it consists in observing the world and formulating truths about it."

So is it true to say that God exists? I would say God exists like love exists, like time exists, like colors exist, like good and evil exist—because all of these are fundamental aspects of human experience. Some of these things, like time and color, can be investigated and represented in scientific terms. Others, like love or a sense of good and evil, can only be known through our experiences and our reasoning about it. They are all "true" in that they shape our daily lives and tell us important things about ourselves and the world we live in. Yet they are not entirely "out there." They all involve some amount of interaction between our bodies and brains and the world around us.

So instead of arguing about whether God "exists," or fighting over whose version of God is "true," I suggest that we explore what it means to live as beings who have a profound sensitivity to what has come to be called the "sacred" or the "Divine." Since at least the beginning of recorded human history, if not earlier, we know that human beings at all times and in all places have had what we can call spiritual experiences. We also know that all human cultures, in a large variety of ways, have developed systems of religious thought and practice to enable people to engage with the cosmos and with one another. To ignore this realm of human experience, to relegate it to random firings of neurons in our brains or dismiss it as superstition, is to overlook a significant part of what makes us human.

Metaphors on the Menu

What I will do in the rest of this book is to explore what is most problematic about our current God metaphors, and the assumptions that so many of us have about what "God" must mean, and then suggest some different ways of thinking about the divine. Each chapter will explore a metaphor that is in many cases very old, yet for us today might seem very new. My hope is that these different God metaphors will make it possible for you, the reader, to reengage with some important spiritual and religious teachings. You may be somewhat comfortable with traditional God language, or be totally turned off by it. Either way, I hope you will enter into this exploration with an open mind and heart.

I am hopeful that this exploration of new ways of thinking about and experiencing the divine will be attractive to people of all backgrounds. My approach to this work

comes from a Jewish perspective, using the texts and traditions that I am familiar with. I will be especially focusing
on metaphors for God that can be found in the Hebrew Bible, for a few reasons. The first is that it is the foundational
text for me as a Jew and as a rabbi, especially the first five
books, which Jewish tradition refers to as the Torah. It is
also a foundational text for Christians, as it makes up (in
slightly different order) the Old Testament, the first part of
the Christian Bible. Stories about and images of God from
the Hebrew Bible have done a great deal to influence how
we think about God in Western culture. Yet at the same
time, many of the biblical metaphors have been lost to us.
The authors of the Hebrew Bible were very closely connected to their land. As such, they experienced the sacred
in ways that may seem more familiar to us from other Indigenous traditions—in earth and fire, in water and sky. In
excavating and resuscitating these biblical metaphors for
God, I hope to offer to people of both Jewish and Christian
heritage, and to anyone of any background who shares this
interest, new ways to approach these holy texts.

I will also be looking at the insights of two thousand
years of Jewish commentators who, in their exploration
of the Hebrew Bible and their own encounters with the
divine, came up with new ways to think about God. In
every era, my rabbinic ancestors have been quite brilliant

at incorporating aspects of their world into the traditions they received. While I can't match their brilliance, I hope to follow their example in weaving together what I find most compelling in Judaism with the realities of the world I live in.

Because my study of new theories of metaphor has shown me that how we think about the world affects how we act, and because I strongly believe that what we believe about God does and should influence our everyday lives, in each chapter I suggest a set of practices to activate a particular metaphor in our lives. These practices are a way of bringing the metaphors off the page and into our lives.

Ultimately, religion is not about a set of beliefs but about how we act and who we are. My hope in coming up with a new "menu" of God metaphors is that once we are properly nourishing our souls, we will be better equipped to live lives that exemplify holy qualities like wisdom, justice, and compassion. Thank you for joining me on this journey.

2
* * * * *

THE GOD METAPHOR

During the Jewish High Holy Days, at Rosh Hashanah and Yom Kippur services, we recite a prayer-poem that was composed during the Middle Ages called the Unetaneh Tokef. It's a complicated piece of liturgy that contemplates human mortality. It begins with the image of God sitting on a throne, reviewing a book that holds the records of our actions. A little farther in, the image shifts to God as a shepherd regarding each member of His flock. Then, in the most memorable part of the prayer, we recite: "On Rosh Hashanah it is written, and on Yom Kippur it is sealed," followed by a litany of possible fates that await us in the new year: who will be enriched and who will become poor, who will thrive and who will suffer, who will live and who will die.

A number of years ago, I met with a congregant who was very troubled by the Unetaneh Tokef. She told me that about ten years earlier, her brother had died very tragically of disease at a young age. After his death, as she sat in Rosh Hashanah services and heard this prayer, she stood up and walked out of the sanctuary. She stayed away from religion for a long time after that.

What this woman heard in the poem was a description of God that she found profoundly troubling. She interpreted the Unetaneh Tokef as saying that somehow her brother's death was his fault; that a distant God sitting on a throne had judged him and sentenced him to a premature death. The idea was so offensive to her that she could no longer bear to attend services.

I personally don't interpret the Unetaneh Tokef in this way, and my congregant and I studied the text together to open up some other possible ways of understanding it. While our conversation made it possible for her to come back to High Holy Days services, at the core of my congregant's strong reaction was a problematic metaphorical understanding of God. And she is not alone. For many people who are uncomfortable with religion generally, and God language specifically, some very powerful assumptions about what belief in God means are grounded in metaphors that we're not even entirely aware of.

I came to understand this in a new way when I read James Geary's description of how different types of metaphors work. In his book *I Is an Other: The Secret Life of Metaphor and How It Shapes the Way We See the World,* Geary outlines a typology of metaphor using the analogy of a volcano's life span: Active, Dormant, and Extinct. In the "Active" category are metaphors that strike us as lively and evocative—for example, the poet Mary Oliver's phrase "the dark hug of time."[1] "Dormant" metaphors are those that we still recognize as metaphors but have become cliché, for example, "I'm up a creek without a paddle." "Extinct" metaphors are those metaphors that we tend to understand as literal truth, forgetting that they are indeed metaphors. The example Geary gives is "I see what you mean."[2] Of course, we don't actually "see" anything when we agree with someone; that's what makes this a metaphor. Underlying this expression is a very common conceptual metaphor, KNOWING IS SEEING, which is based in our experience as infants, who think that something (or someone) ceases to exist when they can't be seen.

What is most powerful about "extinct" metaphors is that they're not really extinct at all. Quite the opposite—we take them so for granted that we think they're describing reality as it is. They are, in the words of Lakoff and Johnson, "metaphors we live by." What I am suggesting here is that for many, many people, God has become an "extinct" metaphor. Regardless of what we say we believe or don't believe, when most of us say the word *God*, what we're referring to is actually a metaphor: GOD IS A BIG POWERFUL PERSON. What we then profess to believe or disbelieve is that metaphor.

Before moving on to think about other possible metaphors for God, I'd like to take a step back and look more closely at the underlying experiences that gave rise to the "extinct" metaphors that dominate our thinking about God, and to explore some of their problematic aspects.

The Religious Imagination

When we talk about God today, we are referring to a set of metaphors that our ancestors began to develop thousands of years ago as they observed their world and formulated truths about it. Human experience of the sacred—that is, a sense of connection to Something beyond our immediate, mundane lives and a desire to interact with that Something—seems to be as old as humanity itself. We see evidence of early humans' sense of spirits or powers beyond this world in remains of burial rituals from as far back as ninety thousand years ago, in cave art from thirty thousand years ago, and in the remains of a temple in Turkey from eleven thousand years ago.[3]

Anthropologist Barbara J. King has suggested that religion evolved in our prehistory as an expression of a fundamental trait she calls "belongingness," which she describes as "a useful shorthand for the undeniable reality that humans of all ages, in all societies, thrive in relation to others."[4] She goes on to say:

> I believe that the desire for emotional connection with the sacred is fundamental to our species . . . The religious imagination thrives on the human yearning to enter into emotional experience with some force vaster than ourselves . . . The human religious imagination developed in ever widening circles of engagement from immediate social companions, to members of a larger group, then across groups, and, eventually, to a wholly other dimension, the realm of sacred beings.[5]

King's use of the term *religious imagination* might imply that religious experience is at base "imaginary," in the sense of "not real." But that is not what King is suggesting. Rather, the ability to "imagine" something beyond ourselves is a highly developed aspect of our brains, which, like conceptual metaphor, is grounded in very real human experiences.

Critics of religion often make the argument that once

upon a time, human beings were unaware of how the world really worked, and saw in natural phenomena like earthquakes, floods, and bounteous harvests the hand of supernatural beings. So, the argument goes, once we have science to explain these things, religion becomes irrelevant and irrational.

But while it may be true that a part of the religious impulse arose from an attempt to understand natural phenomena, humanity's engagement with the sacred has always been about much more than just "explaining things." Our religious and spiritual tendencies are about engaging with all of life, which, for large segments of humanity over the millennia, has also meant engagement with beings or forces—God, gods, or spirits—that lie beyond the human realm. In some cultures, it has included an awareness that all living beings are infused with a sacred life force that must be acknowledged and honored. In others, it has meant shaping one's life in line with a Flow or Way to foster inner qualities like patience, strength, and wisdom. In yet others, it has meant fostering a sense of wonder and awe at the workings of the universe, as well as achieving just and loving relationships among human beings.

A lot of misunderstandings around religion arise because our ancestors thought and wrote in ways that are very different from our modern sensibilities. They thought symbolically, or mythically, and were less interested in what we might call "literal truth" than in larger matters of *meaning*. That is, they told stories not to lay out a list of facts but to get at deeper questions about their own lives and the world around them. Our ancestors expressed their experiences of the realm of the sacred in fairly concrete ways, in stories about divine beings—or a Being—that metaphorically resembled humans and other living creatures. These stories were attempts to understand how the world came to be as it is, and how we can best navigate the world and the various forces that operate within it.

Imagining the divine in these ways not only allowed for mythic narrative; it also allowed for *relationship*. If a god has a name, then we can pray to it and converse with it. If it is imagined to have a form, then we can make a physical representation of it to include in rituals and ceremonies. As Barbara King demonstrates, religious rituals are about relationships: among humans, and between the human realm and the Something that lies beyond it.

God in the Hebrew Bible

Underlying human beings' relationship with the realm of the sacred—expressed in religious rituals and ethical teachings—are conceptual metaphors. In my own tradition, the Hebrew Bible is chock-full of metaphorical imagery of the divine. Like their ancient Near Eastern neighbors, the biblical authors used metaphors from both the human and the natural world to describe how God acts, whether breathing life into Adam, bringing the Israelites out of Egypt on eagles' wings, or appearing in the wilderness as a pillar of cloud. Biblical metaphors for God include Voice, Fire, Warrior, Eagle, Parent, Lawgiver, Water, and many more.[6]

Yet something new and radical for its time and place was the Bible's insistence that we resist the urge to represent God in any physical way. Whatever God was, It could not be contained in any object represented in nature or made by human hands (a major departure from the Mesopotamian and Canaanite cultures that surrounded and influenced the ancient Israelites). While physical imagery could be used in stories about God, when it came to worshipping God, there were to be no statues, no pictures, nothing that a person could point to and say, "There is my God!"

The Hebrew Bible's insistence on no physical images of God seems to have stemmed from a desire to not limit our understanding and experience of the divine.[7] This desire extended to the many metaphors used to depict God in biblical texts. The biblical authors understood that it was impossible to fully describe their experiences of God, and that it took creativity and a plethora of metaphors to capture those experiences. The people who wrote and edited the Bible weren't creating a history textbook or trying to prove a scientific theorem. They were telling stories about the world as they encountered it, and experiences of the divine were a significant part of that encounter.

In his wonderful book *The God of Old,* the biblical scholar James Kugel tries to capture the experience and worldview of the people who wrote the oldest texts within the Hebrew Bible. He investigates stories in which a person suddenly realizes that they are being addressed by a divine being, referred to as a *malakh,* a messenger (this word is often translated as "angel"). In these stories, messengers of God take many forms: a person, a talking donkey, a fire within a bush. At first, the people to whom the messenger appears do not seem to notice anything out of the ordinary (even though we, the readers, do) and then there is what Kugel calls a "sudden *click*" and the person being spoken to realizes that God is present. Kugel writes:

> It is all about perception, something that suddenly opens in the human mind . . . There are not two realms in the Bible, this world and the other, the spiritual and

the material—or rather, these two realms are not neatly segregated but intersect constantly. God turns up around the street corner, dressed like an ordinary person . . . He appears in actual brushfire at the foot of a mountain. And it is not even that, on such occasions, He enters the world as we conceive of it from somewhere else. Rather, it seems that the world itself as we conceive of it (at least the biblical world) has little cracks in it here and there . . . The spiritual is not something tidy and distinct, another order of being. Instead, it is perfectly capable of intruding into everyday reality, as if part of this world.[8]

Kugel's point that biblical narratives about people encountering God are "all about perception, something that suddenly opens in the human mind" is very important. Our biblical ancestors experienced themselves as living in a world in which the realm of the sacred was very near. Accessing this realm had to do with human perceptions, our own ability to see and hear the godly. The issue was not *belief in* God but *experience of* God. Kugel suggests that what we are reading in these stories is "a report on the way things look, on the way it happens."[9] These "reports" take the form of stories, stories that use metaphor to describe an experience that is ultimately beyond the ability of language to fully express.

God as King

I argued earlier that an unspoken, assumed metaphor underlying much of our discussion of God today is the notion that God is a Big, Powerful Person. And while God is never described directly as a Big Person in the Hebrew Bible, there is definitely a lot of metaphoric imagery that supports that notion. Messengers of God often appear looking like ordinary people, and God is described as having human features like a voice and arms, and doing human things like getting angry, talking, and having regrets. The poem in Exodus 15 describing God's triumph over the Egyptian army at the Sea of Reeds speaks of God as a "man of war." Elsewhere in Exodus, we read of Moses talking with God "face to face, as a person speaks to his friend."

In *The God of Old,* Kugel notes that in later parts of the Hebrew Bible, God becomes a more distant power, experienced by people in a less immediate and intimate way compared to the earlier texts. After the destruction of the first Temple in Jerusalem in 586 B.C.E., when the kingdom of Judea was conquered by the Babylonian Empire and the Jewish leadership was exiled to Babylonia, God became increasingly understood as a kind of emperor—distant and very powerful. The Israelite God was now understood to be not just the God of one small nation but the Power that ruled the entire world and used human empires for His own purposes. This imperial God is the basis of the metaphor that most of us assume to be the Jewish (and to a great extent Christian and Muslim) God—the distant, all-knowing, all-powerful King.

But this metaphor is precisely that—just one particular metaphor. It is decidedly *not* the same metaphorical understanding that underlies earlier texts in the Hebrew Bible, where God is never portrayed as all-knowing or all-powerful, in the sense of controlling everything. The "God of old" that Kugel describes is very near, not distant. He/It is unpredictable, showing up at odd times and places, and rarely when expected. He/It is an emotional Being—getting angry, having regrets, changing His/Its mind—as well as compassionate, hearing the cry of the poor and victimized, and promising to respond to suffering. This God is very powerful, but cannot keep humans from doing what they want to do, as the very earliest stories in Genesis attest. In the Garden of Eden, God instructs the first humans to not eat from the Tree of Knowledge of Good and Evil. Eve and then Adam promptly disobey their Creator. In this story, we learn a powerful lesson about human free will, and the limits of God's ability to control Its own creations. Kugel writes that these early texts "seem to be trying to tell us something, something rather sophisticated, about God's very nature—and that something has little to do with the great, omniscient, and omnipresent deity of later times."[10]

What is also important is that along with all this human imagery, there are other biblical depictions of God that are decidedly nonhuman. We are first introduced to God in the Book of Genesis as a "wind that hovers over the waters." In Exodus, we're told that God brings the Israelites out of Egypt "on eagles' wings," and Moses first encounters God as (or somehow within) a burning bush in the desert. In the book of Psalms and throughout the prophetic writings, God is described as life-giving water, as devouring and refining fire, as a rock, as light. Our biblical ancestors employed a breathtaking palette of metaphors to describe their experiences of the sacred. As a tribal people deeply connected to the land, it is not surprising that they used metaphors grounded in their experiences of the natural world.

Thirty-One Flavors

Many years ago, I worked in an ice cream store in Cambridge, Massachusetts. On any given day, we had over twenty flavors of ice cream available, and we were always experimenting with new ones. One day, a father and his young son came into the store. The little boy—not yet able to read—asked his dad, "What flavors are there?" The father looked up at our wonderful list of flavors of the day, and answered, "There's chocolate, vanilla, and strawberry."

While I sympathized with a dad trying to not over-whelm his child with too many choices, I felt so sad for that little boy. Here was a diverse world of marvelous ice cream flavors, hidden from him only because he couldn't read! It's how I feel about most people's experience of God metaphors. If our only flavor choices are "God is a Distant Ruler," or "God is an All-Powerful and Perfect Being That We Can't Really Understand," I'd probably walk out of the store. But the happy reality is that our religious tra-ditions offer the equivalent of Baskin-Robbins's thirty-one flavors when it comes to metaphors for God, and nothing is stopping us from discovering new metaphors that are relevant, powerful, and meaningful to our lives today.

The important thing to remember is that metaphors don't *define* what something is. A metaphor gives us access to an experience, a way to think about it, talk about it, and act on it. To comprehend complex things like "love" or "time" or "ideas," we need multiple metaphors, because any given metaphor will highlight one aspect of a concept and hide other aspects. For example, when we experience time through the metaphor of "precious resource," we tend to think about how much we have and how to best use it. We experience it as limited in some way. But when we think of time as "movement," we relate to it in terms of distances, how far in the past or in the future an event might be. In this understanding, we experience time as endless in both directions. Neither metaphor is "truer" than the other or defines what time actually is; each one simply highlights different aspects of our experience of time.

When it comes to God, the metaphors we use are extremely important, because those metaphors will shape our experience in profound ways, and will affect how we interact with the world around us. As Lakoff and Johnson argue, "New metaphors have the power to create a new reality . . . In most cases, what is at issue is not the truth or falsity of a metaphor but the perceptions and inferences that follow from it and the actions that are sanctioned by it."[11] If we want our spiritual lives to be wholesome, to promote deeper understanding and right action, then the metaphors we use to think and talk about the realm of the sacred are crucial.

As we reexamine ancient metaphors for God and create new ones, we need to be mindful of the implications of each one. What does it hide, and what does it highlight? How might we be encouraged to act in our lives, given a particular way of thinking about God? With multiple metaphors for the divine at hand, we can begin to explore both our own spiritual experiences and the wisdom that has been handed down by our religious traditions.

What Is God For?

There is one last thing to discuss before we begin to look at some different metaphors for God. What are the functions that we need a God metaphor to fulfill? Or to put it another way, what roles have traditional God metaphors played in people's lives, and which of those do we still think are important?

Here are some possibilities to consider (and please feel free to add your own). In many different religious traditions, the divine functions as:

- A source of protection, safety, and refuge
- Creator—that which brought the cosmos into being and keeps it going
- A source of values and ethics—how we know right from wrong

- That which gives us a sense of individual worth (for example, the biblical idea that every human is created "in the image of God")
- That which puts things in perspective—reminding us of our own relative smallness
- The source of obligation—that which demands something of us
- That which enables transformation, the source of freedom and possibility
- The recipient of our gratitude
- That which gives meaning to our lives
- The source of love and compassion—that which supports us and accompanies us in difficult times
- That which provides nourishment for our souls
- The power of life and death itself, the ultimate Mystery

This list has evolved in my discussions with my students, and I am sure there are more that we could add. What I would like to suggest here is that no one metaphor could possibly fulfill all of these functions. It is for precisely this reason that we need a rich palette of God metaphors to enable us to paint as full a picture as possible of how we think about and experience the divine.

A Note About God Language

In the Hebrew Bible and in later Jewish tradition, God has many names. But the one name that is generally viewed as the holiest, the one that somehow holds the essence of God's God-ness, is a name that we don't even know how to pronounce. It contains four Hebrew letters—Yud, Hay, Vav, and Hay—that are all "soft," in the sense that they have no sound without a vowel attached. Some suggest that the sound you get when you put these four letters together is the sound of breath. I will explore this name and its permutations in one of the later chapters; for now, I just want to note that I will sometimes use this name in my discussions of God, using four English letters to stand in for the Hebrew: YHVH. For me, these four letters represent the Ultimate nature of the Divine—that which cannot be fully captured in image, speech, or imagination, yet at the same time is as close—and essential—to us as our breath.[12]

In addition, to wean us away from thinking solely of God in anthropomorphic (human) terms, I will use *It* when referring to the divine with a pronoun (unless I am quoting someone else who might use *He* or *She*). In Hebrew, there is no genderless pronoun like *it*—so every time you see the pronoun *He* used in connection to God in a Bible translation, you could just as correctly use the translation *It*. I know that referring to God as *It* feels very strange to people raised in one of the Abrahamic religions. In my own experience, trying on new language is a helpful exercise in opening up my thinking. I am in no way averse to human metaphors for the divine—there are times when the metaphor of God as Parent, as Beloved, as Teacher, can be powerful and necessary. But in this book, I want to explore different ways of thinking about what God might be, and to do that, we need to push beyond the limitations of human metaphors.

So, with all of that in mind, I invite you to join me on this journey through some new/old metaphors for God.

3
. . . . .

DRINKING FROM GOD

The year that he turned forty, my father suffered a massive heart attack. I remember coming home from school that afternoon (I was in eleventh grade at the time) and being told by my mother what had happened. It was a total shock—my father was young, strong, seemingly healthy. Heart attacks were things that happened on TV, or in the movies, not to me or the people I loved.

Thankfully, my father survived. He spent over a month in the hospital, and came home a different person than the man who went in. After decades of smoking one to three packs of cigarettes a day, he became a virulent nonsmoker. After years of working long hours and subsisting largely on coffee and cigarettes, he pulled way back on the work hours and watched his diet carefully.

But what struck me most as a teenager was the shift in my dad's persona. He was a strong personality and had always had a short temper. He wasn't an abusive parent, but I experienced a lot of yelling and anger in my growing up. The heart attack mellowed him in some significant ways; it seemed to me that he'd had a personality transplant in the hospital. Profoundly shaken at having been brought so close to his own death, my father didn't become religious or even overtly spiritual, but he did take up activities that functioned for him like meditation. Interestingly, the two central activities he chose involved water.

Beginning a few months after he got home from the hospital, he would drive out to the Calvert Cliffs in Maryland, almost an hour from our house, to walk along the beach and collect sharks' teeth and other fossils. He would spend hours there, methodically searching the sand at the base of the cliffs. Wading through the water by the shore, he developed an incredible patience, able to see sharks' teeth lying in the sand that to me were invisible.

At around the same time, my father took up kayaking. This was the late 1970s and early '80s, before paddling became a popular leisure-time activity. To learn how to navigate in white water, my dad took a weeklong course in North Carolina. He would practice rolling his kayak at the local pool. But even though he ended up joining a boat club where Olympic kayakers trained, he wasn't trying to become competitive. He simply loved being out on the Potomac River, whether paddling through flat water or floating down the rapids. And like many recent converts, he was a fervent proselytizer. He would take my brother and me out on the river with him any chance that he got, doing all he could to impart his love of the river to us. He loved to take friends and acquaintances out on the water as well. Long after he'd given up his walks at the Calvert Cliffs, kayaking remained his passion. A few years before his death from a second heart attack at the age of sixty-four, he became president of the American Canoe Association, spreading his gospel of salvation through floating on rivers.

The Bible and Water

I do not think it was entirely coincidental that water-related activities became my father's de facto spiritual practice after his near-death experience. Water is a powerful force of nature, and many people are drawn to spend time by the ocean or by lakes and streams. We owe our very lives to the availability of water; indeed, the majority of our cells are largely made up of water.

In many cultures, water is a symbol of life and power. It is therefore not so surprising that water is one of the most prevalent metaphors for God in the Hebrew Bible. The first association of divinity and water comes in the very first verses of the Creation story, in chapter 1 of Genesis. There we read:

> *At the beginning of God's creating of the heavens and*
> *earth, when the earth was unformed and void, darkness*
> *over the face of the Deep, rushing-spirit of God hovering*
> *over the face of the waters.*[1]

In these somewhat mysterious verses, we read about the *tehom,* usually translated as "the Deep," an unformed, watery primordial mass. Hovering above "the waters" is *ruach Elohim,* which can be translated as "wind" or "spirit" of God. The divine here appears to be surrounded by water, or perhaps It is part of the primordial waters, emerging from the Deep.

Just as current theories of evolution point to our own beginnings in the primordial waters of Earth, three to four billion years ago, so the Torah imagines the beginnings of all of Creation in water. Water is the essential life force, a point made biblically not through scientific theorizing but as part of a story. And God is of the waters, over the waters, active in and through the waters.

As the biblical story continues, water plays an essential role. In the stories of Abraham's family, all of whom dwelt in desert regions of the Near East, water symbolizes welcome and well-being, and often has a connection to people's relationship with God. In Genesis 18, Abraham provides water for his angelic visitors. A little earlier, in chapter 16, Abraham's second wife, Hagar, names a spring of water in honor of her first encounter with YHVH. Water is linked to procreation and the continuity of the family line when Abraham's servant meets his son Isaac's intended, Rebecca, at a well, and again a few chapters later, when Isaac's son Jacob meets his beloved, Rachel, at the very same well.

In the book of Exodus, water imagery is prominent in the Liberation story of the Israelites. Baby Moses is placed into the Nile River by his mother, and rescued from there by Pharaoh's daughter (indeed, the Torah links his name—Moshe in Hebrew—to being drawn out of the water). In a scene that has echoes of birth imagery, the escaping Israelite slaves miraculously walk through a narrow path in the Sea of Reeds, and Moses and his sister, Miriam, lead the people in song and dance on the far shore. If the water of Genesis is linked to creation and sustenance, in Exodus it is symbolic of collective birth and freedom.

Water takes on a new function in the priestly book of Leviticus, where it becomes central to the rituals associated with the Mishkan, the Israelites' portable sanctuary in the desert. When it is time to dedicate his brother and nephew as priests, *"Moses brought Aaron and his sons, and washed them with water.*"[2] The priests must wash themselves before offering sacrifices in the Mishkan, and immersion in water is required for both laypeople and priests who come into contact with any substance that causes them to become ritually impure. Here water is associated not so much with our modern notions of "cleanliness" but with the power to effect spiritual transformation.

In the final book of the Torah, Deuteronomy, water takes on yet another meaning. As the Israelites prepare to enter the promised land—a place very unlike the Egypt they have left, which is sustained by the mighty Nile River—they are told they are coming to *"a good land, a land of brooks of water, of streams and springs that flow out of valleys and hills."*[3] Those streams and springs are dependent on the seasonal rainfall, without which the land will dry up and the crops will fail. In the theology of the Deuteronomic writers, rainfall is a sign of God's blessing, and is linked to the Israelites' faithfulness to the covenant.

The importance of water in these biblical narratives gives us a rich sense of what water meant to its authors (and presumably its early readers): water is essential, life-giving, a symbol of both Creation and Liberation, purifying, and a conduit of godly blessing. All of these are qualities that can be associated as well with divinity, with That which creates and sustains the world.

Drinking from God

I grew up in Maryland, where access to water was never an issue. There was plenty of rain year-round, and so much humidity in the summer you could practically drink the air. Then, at the age of eighteen, I went to spend a year in Israel, living on a kibbutz in the Negev desert. Suddenly, water was a precious resource. Rain only fell in the winter months, and in the orchards where I worked, the trees were sustained by miles of drip irrigation tubes. It was hot but dry in the summer, and we Americans had to be constantly reminded to drink. I remember our first hike in the desert, stopping to take a drink from my canteen. I didn't even realize, until the water hit my mouth, how incredibly thirsty I was. It is hard to express how deeply satisfying that canteen of lukewarm water was in that moment.

That experience comes to mind as I read biblical passages where the author speaks of thirsting for God, and drinking from a godly well or stream:

How precious is Your love, O God! . . . Humanity is nourished from the riches of Your house, You give them drink from the stream of your delight.

Elohim, You are my God; I seek You, my soul thirsts for
You; my flesh faints for You, as in a dry and weary land
where there is no water.

As the deer longs for water streams, so does my soul
long for You, O God. My soul thirsts for God, for the
living God.[4]

When I think of my father walking along the water's edge
by the Calvert Cliffs, or paddling on the Potomac, I wonder
if his soul was drinking in some kind of spiritual sustenance,
even as his physical self was enjoying the literal waters. I
know that this metaphor of a "thirsty soul" resonates with
me. It is an accurate description of those times when I feel
spiritually dry, as if some essential source of nourishment
has been cut off. In those moments, I am like that deer in the
Judean desert, searching for an *afik,* a channel in the earth
that fills when it rains. At these times, God is the Source
from which my thirsty soul can be quenched, if only I am
willing to drink. In the words of the prophet Isaiah, I can be
like that orchard in the Negev, nourished by godly waters:

YHVH shall guide you always, and satisfy your soul in
drought . . . and you shall be like a watered garden.[5]

God as Water

As I first began looking for metaphors for God in the Bible, I was astonished at the abundance of water images. In addition to the images of God "watering" the people like a garden, and the spiritual seeker desiring to "drink" from God, I discovered what I call *water names* for the divine. In the book of Isaiah, we find this passage:

> *Here, God of my liberation, I will trust and not be afraid; for Yah YHVH is my strength and my song, and has been my liberation. Joyfully you shall draw water from the Well of Liberation.*[6]

Here God is described as the prophet's *"yeshua,"* which can be translated as "liberation" or "salvation." Isaiah then instructs us to "draw water from the well of *yeshua*"—referring back to this experience of God as liberation. "Well of Liberation" is a beautiful metaphor for the Divine—an endless source from which we can draw and drink. What "liberation" or "salvation" might mean is left up to us. I like to think of it as liberation from suffering, from the internal struggles that confine me as well as the external challenges I face. To draw upon the Well of Liberation is to have access to Something beyond me—and deep within me—which I can have faith is always there, even when I'm not entirely aware of it. Like finding water in a well, I may need to dig to access this sense of liberation, to search deep within myself to draw it up.

In the book of Jeremiah, we find a different water name for God, in a verse where the prophet excoriates the people for going astray:

> *For my people have committed two evils; they have forsaken Me, the Fount of Living Waters, and dug cisterns for themselves, broken cisterns, which can hold no water.*[7]

"Fount of Living Waters"—what a beautiful metaphor for That which sustains us spiritually! Here the prophet warns of seeking nourishment from "broken cisterns," from those things (and they are usually things) that we mistakenly believe can nourish our spirits—perhaps money, or fame, or accumulating stuff. In this metaphor, God is the living, accessible spring without which we cannot live. In the Psalms, YHVH is referred to as *River of Bliss* and *River of God,*[8] images of the divine as an overflowing source of abundance, nourishment, and delight.

In thinking about God as Water, the first thing I notice is how different the verbs describing godly action are in contrast to God as Big, Powerful Person. Water does not command or judge—it flows and irrigates, nourishes and sustains. God as Water invites us to identify when and how we become spiritually "dry," and what it might mean to feel spiritually nourished. The divine can be found in those activities or experiences that function as our own "well of salvation."

And unlike God as Distant Emperor, God as Water is not "out there," far from us, but right here, within us. In the first chapter of Genesis, we are told that human beings are created *b'tzelem Elohim*, "in God's image." About 70 percent of the human body is made up of water; our brains and hearts are approximately 80 percent water.[9] What new meaning the phrase "made in God's image" takes on if we think of God as Water, and ourselves as made up largely of that godly substance! We are literally composed of sacred stuff. Water is precious and powerful and essential, as are we.

Troubled Waters

I found the metaphor of God as Water to be enormously helpful during some of the most challenging months of my life. In the spring of 2014, my spouse, Gina, was diagnosed with metastatic breast cancer. After a year of experimental treatments in which she was relatively symptom-free, in the fall of 2015 things took a turn for the worse, and she died the following March. Those months leading up to her death, during which she endured a nasty course of chemotherapy, were profoundly difficult. I needed every ounce of strength and compassion I could find to be a support to Gina and to keep from being overwhelmed by sadness and despair. During this journey, I found myself drawn to a chant composed by my colleague and teacher, Rabbi Shefa Gold, a setting of a verse from the book of Isaiah:

When you pass through the waters, I am with you; I won't let the rivers overwhelm you.[10]

Chanting these words, I realized the profound insight of this verse. As I struggled to understand where God was in the terrible reality I was facing, I realized that water is essential to life—indeed, water *is* life—and yet sometimes it is also That which threatens me, overwhelms me, drowns me. God was at one and the same time the waters through which I was passing, and That which supported me as I made my way through an unbearable reality.

Facing the prospect of the death of my beloved, I didn't rail against the unfairness of an inscrutable God who had brought suffering into my life. Instead, in the slow-motion heartbreak of that terrible year, I did my best to sit with the reality that ultimately faces each and every one of us. I remembered my father's instruction to lean *into*, not away from, the turbulence when navigating a kayak through the rapids. I understood that the waves can be overwhelming and terrifying, and yet within them is the godly Presence that sustains and supports me, even in the most difficult moments. I gave myself over to overwhelming waters, allowing myself to feel the profound sorrow within them, even as I sought the reassurance of God's Presence accompanying me as I made my way down the river.

The Power of Water

When I was a teenager, in the Dark Ages before mobile phones and the internet, it was challenging to stay in touch with faraway friends. The summer after eleventh grade, I went to camp and met kids from my youth movement who lived all over the country. Back home, I wanted to stay in touch with them, but long-distance telephone calls were prohibitively expensive. One of my friends had figured out how to charge calls to a third party, and she'd found a list of phone numbers of embassies of particularly odious regimes. Feeling like I was both avoiding a huge expense and striking a blow for justice, I would head out to the local 7-Eleven, which had a pay phone outside, and spend hours talking with my far-flung friends, charging the calls to a variety of Latin American dictatorships.

One day, my mother found out what I had been doing. My mom is the most honest person I know, and she was incredibly upset by this. In my rather obnoxious teenage way, I didn't understand what was so wrong. "It's not like these embassies can't afford it, and besides, they're terrible!" But my protestations were to no avail. It was dishonest, it was stealing, and my mother insisted that she'd rather pay for the calls herself than have me continue.

I think I stopped at that point, most immediately because I was afraid of getting caught. But on a deeper level, I was moved by my mother's commitment to her values. She didn't punish me, but she taught me something that I still remember.

I wonder about the sense of obligation that each of us feels in different ways, obligations to other people, to a sense of right and wrong, to deeply held values. Each of us has lines that we won't cross. For my mother, I had clearly crossed the line with my third-party phone calls. I have many such lines in my own life. I became a vegetarian at age thirteen because I didn't want to harm animals. I won't cross a picket line of striking workers. I always tell a cashier if they haven't charged me properly. Some people think of these types of obligations as coming from their parents, or from some innate sense of right and wrong. For others, ethical dos and don'ts come directly from God. For many people, a central role of religion is to make clear what is right and wrong, and to back it up with a divine decree.

In the Hebrew Bible, the metaphor that most people think of when it comes to telling right from wrong is God as King, the Commander in Chief who lays down the law for His subjects. The whole point of Moses freeing the Israelites from slavery in Egypt and schlepping them across the desert was to bring them to Mount Sinai, where they received the Ten Commandments and entered into a covenantal relationship with YHVH. This relationship entailed a whole set of ritual and ethical laws governing the Israelites' behavior toward one another and toward the divine Power that had liberated them. In the ancient Near East, this idea of a community entering into a covenant with God was a radical new idea. Most of the surrounding cultures attributed godlike powers to the local human ruler, and treated his laws as if they were divine. The authors of the Torah said no, there is a Power above all human rulers, and His word is the ultimate law. Even a king has to obey that law.

But what happens when we no longer believe in a Ruler-Commander God? Does that mean that our sense of right and wrong is random and relative, differing from person to person based on our idiosyncratic upbringings? Is there anything "out there" that obligates us, and if so, how?

To answer those questions, we need to return to the metaphor of God as Water, and go to the final book of the Torah, Deuteronomy. This book consists of a series of monologues spoken by Moses to the Israelite people as they stand on the bank of the Jordan River, waiting to cross into the promised land. It's been forty years since they left Egypt, and Moses knows that he won't be accompanying the people into Canaan. The words of Deuteronomy are his final words of inspiration, warning, and instruction. He exhorts the Israelites every way he knows how to abide by the obligations of the covenant that they entered into at Sinai. In one important passage, speaking on behalf of God, Moses uses a powerful water metaphor to make his point:

> *Now it shall be, if you truly listen to My instructions that I command you today, to love YHVH your God and to serve God with all your heart and with all your being, I will give you the rain of your land in its due-time, early rain and later rain, that you may gather in your grain, your wine, and your oil . . . Beware lest your heart be deceived, and you turn away and serve other gods, bowing down to them, and YHVH's anger will be against you, and the skies will*

close and there will be no rain, and the earth will not yield
its produce, and you will soon be lost from the good land
that YHVH is giving to you.[11]

Often these verses are understood as a literal statement
of reward and punishment. Rainfall was essential to the
people's well-being in the land of Canaan, so the threat of
no rain was a serious one. It's as if God is saying, "If you
keep my commandments, then you'll receive the blessing
of rain, and if not, I'll make you suffer."

If we assume that GOD IS A POWERFUL RULER,
then the reward-and-punishment interpretation makes sense.
Reward and punishment are key components of a system
based on coercive power, a power *over* others, the ability to
make those who are less powerful do what we want. This
is often the main kind of power associated with God—and
for many, it is this view of divine power that is the most
problematic. Why would we want to think of God as essentially a tyrant coercing people to do things they don't
want to do? And if this tyrannical power is the kind that
God wields, why isn't the world a better place? Are all the
terrible things that happen to us a punishment from God?

But if we think of God as the "Fount of Living Waters,"
we can read these verses quite differently. Instead of reward

and punishment, we can understand the Torah to be describing a *sacred ecology of actions and their consequences.* In this ecology, the flow of water is key to understanding our relationship with the Source of Life. By fulfilling our spiritual and ethical obligations, we align ourselves with a Divine Flow of goodness and truth. When we do this, "the rain falls," the waters of nourishment and blessing pour out as they are meant to.*

What Deuteronomy describes as God's "anger" can be understood, in the water metaphor, as being shut off from the Divine Flow. This happens not as a punishment but as an inherent consequence of our actions. We experience a drought, an absence of godly blessing, when we ignore our obligations to ourselves, to one another, to the earth, and to our divine Source. We might feel this drought personally, as a kind of spiritual crisis, or we might experience it as an entire society, in the economic, political, and environmental realms.

In the metaphor of God as Water, we are given a whole new way to think about God's power, and how that power affects us. Water's impact is felt in a myriad of ways: in the sweeping destruction of a tidal wave, in the slow wearing away of stones in a river, in the creation of massive canyons

---

* My teacher Rabbi Arthur Waskow first brought to my attention this understanding of the flow of divine blessing in the Torah.

through eons of steady pressure. Water's power can be deadly and overwhelming, but it can also be subtle and gentle.

The power contained in the ocean's tide or the flow of a river flow is akin to what some theologians call *persuasive power.* Unlike coercive power, which forces us to do something against our will, persuasive power orients us and encourages us to move in a certain direction. This kind of power works not by diminishing us or crushing our will but by showing us how to come into our fullest and best selves. Persuasive power can be more or less forceful, just like a river's current can be gentle or knock us off our feet. It cajoles and instructs, challenges and inspires. My mother's anger with me about the long-distance phone calls exhibited just this sort of persuasive power, urging me to do what was right, even if I thought there was some short-term benefit in doing wrong.

If we think about Godly power using water metaphors—as an ocean, a stream, a driving rain—we can move beyond a concept of power as "control over," and let go of the notion of God as some kind of puppet master. We will also have to let go of any fantasy of God as a superhero who will show up and save the day when evil threatens us. God as Cosmic Flow can show us the way and guide our path, but only if and when we are willing to channel that Power for the good.

Rain of Justice

The biblical scholar Klaus Koch has argued that for the Hebrew prophets, the biblical concepts of *mishpat* (justice) and *tzedakah* (righteousness) were actual forces in the universe, sort of like gravity. These forces were often described as fluids, as rivers and rain, with YHVH as their source. Proper human action would cause the "rain of justice" to fall; improper action would have the opposite effect.[12]

The prophet Isaiah excoriates the leaders of Jerusalem for their ethical failings, describing it as a city *"where righteousness dwelt, but now murderers,"* where the leaders fail to bring justice for the powerless, the widow and the orphan. Because of this, they *"shall be like an oak with wilting leaves, and like a garden that has no water."*[13] After powerful words of critique against those who abuse their power, who oppress their workers and exploit the poor, Isaiah goes on to promise that if his listeners clothe the naked and provide housing for the destitute, then *"YHVH will guide you always, and satisfy your soul in parched places. . . . You shall be like a watered garden, like a spring whose waters do not fail."*[14]

A more recent prophet, Dr. Martin Luther King Jr., made

famous a verse from the book of Amos, where justice is explicitly likened to water: *"Let justice well up like water, and righteousness like a flowing stream."*[15] And in the book of Hosea, we read, *"It is time to seek YHVH, until it comes and rains down justice upon you."*[16] Indeed, the biblical word for the early winter rain, *yoreh*, comes from the same root as the word *Torah*, meaning "instruction" or "teaching." How do we learn to do what is right? By creating vessels—spiritual practices, social policies—that can hold the nourishing rain of justice. How do we fulfill our obligations to those around us? By aligning ourselves with the flow of a godly river that moves us in the direction of love and righteousness. It is up to us whether we will swim in harmony with the "flowing stream" that Amos describes, or fight the current.

It is important to note that in these passages, the "you" to whom the prophets are speaking is a collective "you," the people of Israel as a whole and/or its leadership. The lack of rain doesn't happen to individual farmers but to the society as a whole. A corrupt leader or oppressive business person might individually profit in the short term, but the consequences of injustice will ultimately be felt by all. These consequences include both a state of spiritual drought and devastation in the world around us. Today, as we reckon with the very real effects of climate change—much of it caused by our insatiable human greed and out-of-control consumerism—the ecological consequences of our collective moral and spiritual crisis are beyond what the biblical authors could ever have imagined.

Planting Justice, Harvesting Love

The model of a sacred ecology of actions and consequences, an outgrowth of the metaphor of God as Water, provides us with a powerful way to think about the creation of a more just and loving world. Often, in the realm of politics and social change, we operate within metaphors of war and sports. We need to take a "side," and our objective is to defeat those whom we oppose. There are winners and losers, "good guys" and "bad guys." Just as in the military or on a sports team, it is important to define who is "in" and who is "out," with a need for uniforms—of thought and practice—to define who is who.

There are times when the war/sports metaphors are useful and appropriate. People running a campaign to elect a candidate or pass new laws need to strategize and win, just like a successful football team. And I have certainly had moments—like when striking workers are picketing their employer during a labor dispute—when I have needed to choose a "side" and support those workers by not crossing that line. But there are also real dangers in this metaphorical model. The assumption that there must be "winners" and "losers" implies that if justice is done for one group of people, then others will of necessity be on the losing end. The need to define "sides" often leads to the demonization of those whose opinions or experiences don't fit into the "uniform" of our team. And there are many issues we face that don't easily fall into the binary of "good guys" versus "bad guys." Life is often quite a bit messier than that.

What happens when we immerse ourselves instead in an ecological model?

The first thing I think about is that there are no "teams" or "sides" in the natural world. Instead, all forms of life interact with and affect one another. An imbalance in one place can have repercussions far away. Poisons that get into the ecosystem upstream will ultimately have disastrous effects downstream. Ultimately, there are no "winners" or "losers," just healthy or unhealthy systems, in which everything is affected for good or for bad.

In this model, if I want to align myself with the Divine flow of justice and love, then I have to understand the effects my actions—or inaction—have on the world around me. I need to pay attention to the sea in which I swim, and notice what I am absorbing in the air I breathe. What harmful attitudes and assumptions are simply part of the ecosystem in which I live? And once I become aware of them, what do I need to do?

For example: as a white person, the ecological model invites me to understand racism as a deeply embedded toxin in the society I inhabit. As a foundational force in America since the very beginnings of European settlement, ideas about white supremacy have shaped the social structures around me and are embedded in my brain, in the form of unconscious bias. I am a product of my environment, just like everyone else. Given that reality, I am not a "bad guy" when I inevitably say or do something that exhibits racism. I don't need to demonize other white people in order to prove that I really am on the side of the angels. Instead, I can explore the ways in which systemic racism has benefited me, even as it has severely harmed Black and brown people around me. I can also explore the very real ways that racism has harmed me and those I love. Once I understand that harm, I realize that the entire system is damaged, that a toxin lives within me, and that I have both self-interest and a moral obligation to remove the toxin of racism from the ecosystem that I inhabit. I can then commit to the work of making change, both inside myself and in the world around me. I can do this with an awareness that I will most likely make mistakes—and then try again. I can learn what it means to be in solidarity with people of color, and how I can be a part of efforts to remove the toxic waste of racism from the world in which I live. No one loses, and everyone wins, if those efforts are successful.

The prophet Hosea teaches: *"Plant justice for yourselves, harvest according to lovingkindness; till the untilled ground, and a time to seek YHVH, until it rains down justice for you."*[17] Like a farmer following the plow, I can aspire to plant seeds of justice with every step that I take. Like a worker in the fields, I can harvest loving-kindness by opening my heart to as many people as possible, and by having some compassion on myself and others when we fall short of our aspirations. The world around us is "untilled ground," just waiting for us to do the holy work that will bring down the nurturing rains of healing for all.

God as Water Practice

Beautiful images of God as Water abound in our sacred texts, yet over the millennia they have become stuck to the page, lifeless. To give this metaphor the power to shape our experience, we need to actively engage the images and bring them back to life—to connect them to our own lived experiences of water. What follows are a series of practices that you can try to do just that. I use the word *practice* advisedly; like anything else, developing a new spiritual language takes time and effort. It is not easy to dislodge old God metaphors and open the mind and heart to new ones, but in my experience, it is well worth the effort. I invite you to try each of these for a few weeks, and see what happens.

Chant: Biblical metaphors for God are, in a way, like dried soup mix, just needing hot water to transform into something delicious and nourishing. Take, for example, Psalm 42, an extended meditation on God as Water:

> *As the deer longs for water streams, so does my soul long for You, O God. My soul thirsts for God, for the living God . . . When I remember these things, I pour out my soul . . . Deep calls to Deep in the roar of your waterfalls; all your waves and breakers have swept over me.*

There are so many powerful images here: the deer— representing the soul—longing for water; the soul thirsting for the Living God; the Deep (of God?) calling out to the Deep (in us?); the feeling of godly waves and breakers sweeping over us. The practice of sacred chant is one way to reactivate these texts, to bring them back to life. Rabbi Shefa Gold writes of this practice:

Chanting is the melodic and rhythmic repetition of a Hebrew phrase drawn from our sacred text. It is a practice that allows for the exploration of the deeper levels of meaning and experience that lie beneath the surface of our religious lives . . . Chant is a practice that connects the outer dimensions of sound . . . with the inner dimensions of awareness . . . When we chant, we are using the whole body as the instrument with which to feel the meaning of the sacred phrase.[18]

On her website, Rabbi Gold has links to chants that she has written for many of the verses that I've cited in this chapter (plus many more). Here are just a few that you can find there:

Just as the deer longs for water by the riverbank
So does my soul long for You, oh God
Ken nafshi ta'arog aylecha Elohim
(Psalm 42:2—https://www.rabbishefagold.com/longing-kayn-nafshi/)

All of Your breakers and Your waves have swept
    over me
Kol mish'barecha v'galecha alai avaru
(Psalm 42:8—https://www.rabbishefagold.com/pure/)

My soul thirsts for God, for the Living God
Tzam'ah nafshi l'Elohim l'El Chai
(Psalm 42:3—https://www.rabbishefagold.com
/encountering-living-god/)

All who are thirsty, come for water!
Hoy! Kol tzamay l'chu lamayim
(Isaiah 55:1—https://www.rabbishefagold.com/come
-for-water/)

Choose a chant that you would like to explore. First spend a little time with the words of the chant, seeing what they bring to mind (on Rabbi Gold's website, there is an introduction to each chant and its deeper meanings). Close your eyes, and take a moment to bring your attention to the breath. Then, try singing the chant for anywhere between ten and twenty minutes (the longer, the better). Once the chant becomes familiar, you might find that you are no longer thinking about it, but letting it chant itself.

When you finish chanting, sit for a moment or two in the silence that follows. See what arises. What feelings has the chant evoked? What longings, or fears, or pleasures? Perhaps there are no strong feelings, which is fine; there is nothing particular that is supposed to happen. But keep at it, and see what a few weeks of engaging with these images brings into your life. Take this as an opportunity to explore your own sense of being spiritually "dry" and spiritually nourished, and to experience God as a Divine Flow through which you are "watered" and sustained.

Water Blessings: In Jewish practice, it is traditional to say a blessing both when we wash our hands before eating and when we drink water. Saying blessings is in essence a mindfulness practice—an opportunity to pause before a mundane act and to become fully present to the daily miracles with which we are blessed. Given the extent to which many of us take water for granted in our lives, pausing to note our encounters with water is a wonderful opportunity to connect it—and ourselves—back to the sacred Source, the Fount of Living Waters.

The Hasidic teacher Rabbi Shlomo of Karlin (1740–1792) offered this as an intention for handwashing:

> You should think that in this water also there is the life-power of God; and if it were not there the water would pass out of existence. Think of this water as linked to its spiritual root, which is the spiritual water, the pure water that purifies; and that is what this water signifies.[19]

Make a point of mindfully washing your hands before each meal, and/or upon awakening and before going to bed at night. Pay attention as you feel the water on your hands—the physical sensation, the sound. Using Rabbi Karlin's words as a guide, imagine "the life-power of God" within the water as you feel it on your hands; imagine both the physical and the "spiritual water" bathing you and connecting to the physical and spiritual water of which you are made.

Similarly, you can take those times during the day when you drink water as an opportunity for reflection and blessing. Here is an adapted Hebrew blessing, to be said before you drink:

> *Nevarekh it eyn hachaim m'kor mayyim chayim*—Let us
> bless the Source of life, Fount of Living Waters.

Prayer and God as Water: If you have a prayer practice, you can experiment with using water names for God as part of that practice. Some names that the Bible suggests include:

- Well of Liberation—*Ma'ayan Hayeshua*
- River of God—*Peleg Elohim*
- Fount of Living Waters—*M'kor Mayyim Chayim*
- Faithful Waters—*Mayyim Ne'emanu*
- Torrent of Delight—*Nachal Adanecha*
- Deep—*Tehom*

If you are using traditional Jewish liturgy, you can substitute any of these names for YHVH. Or for anyone of any background, you can try praying to, or entering into conversation with, the Deep or the Torrent of Delight or the Fountain of Living Waters. See where your soul is "thirsty," and what you might ask of the Deep/Torrent/Fountain to help quench that thirst. See if you can sense godliness within you, in the water that fills your cells, that bathes you on the inside.

The Power of Water: Practice

If we think of God as a mighty river flowing in the direction of justice and love, then one key component of spiritual practice is to place ourselves in alignment with that flow. If we resist, there will be consequences—akin to trying to swim upstream against a mighty current. Sometimes the direction of the flow is obvious, and when we swim against it, the consequences are immediate. Those times in my life when I have spoken in anger or said hurtful things to another person, I usually know right away that I've made a mistake—either due to the other person's reaction, or my own sense of shame and remorse.

But often the flow is subtle, and we need a great deal of discernment to know how to navigate it. Ethical dilemmas are not always easy to resolve, and right action is not always clear. One way to understand spiritual practice is as a process of aligning ourselves with the godly Flow of the universe, in order to gain insight into what each moment asks of us, and to know best how to respond. "Doing the right thing" becomes a process of navigation, with all of the twists and turns that that implies.

Going with the flow: To navigate a river, it is helpful to know where I am, and to have some sense of where I would like to go. Here are two exercises you can do to help achieve alignment between your deepest commitments and the way you lead your life:

- **Where am I?** You can begin by taking some time to clarify what you believe to be your most fundamental values. What do you really care about—in your own life, in the world around you? Think of the people you truly admire, and note the qualities that define who they are. Then, do a bit of accounting: write down where you spend the majority of your time and your money. Compare your list of values with your time/money account. How much of your resources go to the things you say you most care about? If "family" is at the top of your list of values, but you spend most of your time at work and very little with your spouse or kids or other dear ones, then something is out of alignment.

Similarly, if you say that you value generosity, or
making change in the world, but realize that you spend
90 percent or more of your discretionary income—or
most of your free time—on your own pleasure, then
something may be out of whack. The idea is not that
you need to deny yourself or live like a saint; it is to say
that sometimes we have an idea of ourselves that is not
in line with what we actually do. This alignment exercise is one way to get a clearer picture of whether your
resources and actions are aligned with your values—
and if not, then you have an opportunity to begin to
make some course corrections.

- **Where am I going?** One of the most useful exercises I
ever did as a thirty-year-old rabbinical school student
was writing my own obituary. It was a wonderful invitation to think about what I hoped people would say
about me when I'm gone. Writing our own obituary or
eulogy is an opportunity to clarify what we want our
lives to be about. For example, in American society,
there is a lot of attention and adulation given to people
who make enormous amounts of money. Yet after more
than twenty-five years of doing funerals, I can honestly
say that not once have I been asked to announce how
much money the deceased person made in their life,
how many houses they owned, or the net worth of

their investment portfolio. And those times when I've met with mourners who have struggled to find positive words to say about the deceased are truly heartbreaking. So write your obituary, and see if you can be both visionary and realistic. Do you want to be remembered for how you interacted with the people around you? For the change you made in the lives of others? For your art, or your generosity, or how you cared for the earth or for your family and friends? Once the obituary is written, think of it as a destination on your journey. How will you get there? Are you already on course, or do you need to make a few maneuvers to make sure you're making your way down the right stream?

Activating Torah: The biblical metaphor of God as the source of the flow of justice and right living opens up powerful ways of thinking and acting in the world. To make these images more than just interesting words on a page, we need to "activate" the metaphor in our own minds and hearts. This technique comes from a Jewish tradition called Mussar, a collection of ethical practices and teachings that have developed over the past one thousand years. I am indebted to my friend and teacher Rabbi David Jaffe for introducing me to this practice:

Choose a verse that you would like to explore more

deeply. In the selections below, I have offered English translations that are as close to the Hebrew as possible. If you are
more familiar with the King James Version, or are comfortable with Hebrew, please use whatever version works best
for you. If you are near a body of water, try this practice outside by a lake or stream or the ocean. If you're inside, find
some sounds of flowing water online as the background to
your exploration. Being in the presence of the sight and/or
sound of living water helps bring the verses to life.

1. Step 1: Begin by studying the verse. What images does
   it call to mind? What qualities of water do you think it is
   referring to? If the verse does not make sense when you
   first read it, see if you can figure out what it might be
   trying to say. You can do this alone, or you might want
   to find a study partner to help you wrestle with the text.
2. Step 2: See if you can relate the verse to your life. What
   justice issue is on your mind lately? Where are you
   feeling injustice, or a lack of loving-kindness or peace?
   Where are you feeling called to take action? What is
   holding you back from taking action?
3. Step 3: Bring the text to life by engaging with it out
   loud. Speak it, chant it, sing it, shout it, whisper it. Play
   with it, ask questions of it. Do this for at least ten to fifteen minutes. See what new insights you gain when you

try to bring the meaning of the verse into your heart.
Let yourself be surprised!

Verses for practice:

*If only you would listen to My instructions, then your
    peace/well-being (shalom) would be like a river, and
    your justice as the waves of the sea.* (Isaiah 48:18)

*For my people have committed two evils; they have for-
    saken Me, the fount of living waters, and dug cisterns
    for themselves, broken cisterns, that can hold no
    water.* (Jeremiah 2:13)

*Plant justice for yourselves, harvest according to loving-
    kindness; till the untilled ground, and a time to seek
    YHVH, until it rains down justice for you.* (Hosea
    10:12)

*Children of Zion, be glad and rejoice in YHVH your
    God; for God has given you the rain of instruction
    for justice.* (Joel 2:23)

*Let justice well up like water, and righteousness like an
    ever-flowing stream.* (Amos 5:24)

*Here, God of my liberation, I will trust and not be
    afraid; for Yah YHVH is my strength and my song,
    and has been my liberation. Joyfully you shall draw
    water from the wells of liberation.* (Isaiah 12:2–3)

4

· · · · ·

HOW AWESOME
IS THIS PLACE

Jacob is on the run. He has created an awful mess with his family, tricking his father, Isaac, into giving him a blessing that had been intended to go to his twin brother, Esau. When Jacob's mother, Rebecca, heard Esau swear to murder his brother, she convinced Isaac to send Jacob away, ostensibly to seek a wife back in Rebecca's hometown of Haran.

So Jacob sets out for Haran. He comes upon a place which seems to be no place, with no distinguishing features other than some rocks. As night approaches, he takes one of the rocks as a pillow and has a wild dream. In the dream, there is a ladder extending from the earth to the heavens, with messengers of God traveling up and down it. All of a sudden, God Godself is standing right next to Jacob, and gives him a promise: the land on which he is lying will be given to his descendants, who will be as numerous as the dust of the earth, and he, Jacob, will receive divine protection throughout his journey. Jacob awakens from the dream and exclaims, "There is YHVH in this place, and I didn't know! How awesome is this place." Jacob consecrates the place, calling it Beit-El, "House of God."

This intriguing story unfolds in just a few verses in chapter 28 of the Book of Genesis. Upon closer inspection, it appears that this story is very carefully constructed, with some important repetitions of key words, offering us clues about its meaning.

In verse 11, we find the Hebrew word meaning "the place"—*ha-makom*—repeated three times:

Jacob encountered *the place*
He took one of the stones *of the place*
He lay down *in that place*

Then in verses 12–15, we read about the dream, and the words for *earth* and *soil* are repeated a number of times. Finally, in verses 16–19, the word for *place* is repeated three times again:

Jacob awoke and said:
YHVH is in *this place*

How awesome is *this place!*
And he called *the name of the place Beit El / House of God.*

All in all, in the space of just nine verses, the word for "place," *makom* (pronounced mah-COMB)—is repeated six times. This is a clue that this word is very important. The repetition in the dream of the words for *earth* and *soil* is also a clue. So what can we make of all of this repetition?

When Jacob first encounters the "place," it seems nondescript—just a rocky field in the middle of nowhere. After his dream, Jacob has a totally different understanding of "the place." Now he realizes that "God is in this place," and "how awesome is this place!" He goes on to say that "this is none other than the house of God, this is a gateway to heaven." As readers, we are left to wonder whether this particular "place" was always special, or if it became holy because of the experience that Jacob had there—an experience that could, presumably, have happened in any "place."

The repetitions in the verses about the dream emphasize the earthiness of Jacob's experience. While the dream features a ladder that reaches into the sky, and while Jacob understands "the place" to be a gateway to the heavens, the words describing his dream point repeatedly to the earth, to the rocks and the dirt on which he is lying. This profound experience of God's presence doesn't happen up at the top of the ladder but down here on the ground.

Jacob is in a very vulnerable situation when he has this dream. I imagine him as afraid and uncertain, and perhaps feeling a bit guilty as well. He has left behind everything he knows, without any idea of when he might return. It is in this emotional and psychic "place" that this marvelous encounter with God—his first—occurs. Perhaps the Torah is trying to tell us that a godly encounter is possible in any place, if we are open to it. While we might associate the divine with "up there" in heaven, this story seems to be telling us that we can find It a lot closer, right here in the place where we are, even when (especially when?) that "place" is a difficult one.

God as "Place"

There are places I'll remember
All my life though some have changed
Some forever, not for better
Some have gone and some remain

—John Lennon and Paul McCartney, "In My Life"

When I was in elementary school, I spent a lot of time in the woods near my house. Along with my dog, I would climb on rocks in the streambed, walk along the paths, and sit under trees and make up songs. It was a fairly small woods, surrounded by houses and even some high-rise apartments, but in certain spots and at certain seasons, I could pretend I was off in an expansive forest, far from civilization. The woods were my refuge, my creative place, a kind of second home. Thinking back, I'm somewhat amazed at how much time I could spend there. To this day, my soul feels nourished when I'm in the woods, surrounded by trees, listening to a stream as it rushes over stones.

This is the power of place, whether it's the woods or a bedroom, a summer camp or a beloved classroom. Each of us can, like the Beatles song says, conjure up places that have played a special role in our lives. I can still remember the moment—and the look on his face—when I took my then eleven-year-old nephew to Fenway Park for the first time. Each time I visit Israel, I encounter smells and visceral sensations that take me back to my first time living there, when I was eighteen. If I think back to all the places I've lived over the course of my life, whether for years or a few months, each functions as a memorable way station on this journey of my life.

When I ask people to tell me about their God beliefs, often they have no idea what to say, or simply say they don't believe in God. But if I ask them to describe a spiritual experience that they've had, whatever that may mean to them, many will tell me about special places in their lives.

So perhaps it shouldn't be so surprising that by the early rabbinic period (the first two centuries of the Common Era), the epithet *HaMakom*—"The Place"—had become a fairly well-known Jewish name for God. In the Mishnah, the earliest compilation of rabbinic teachings, there are instructions for prayer that include this comment: "The ancient pious ones would meditate for an hour and then pray, in order to direct their heart to *HaMakom* / The Place."[1] Another early teaching is recorded in the Talmud, in a discussion of what to say to people who are ill: "Rabbi Judah would say, 'May *HaMakom* / The Place have compassion upon you and all who are sick.'"[2]

But what exactly does it mean to call God "the Place"? What are we to make of this metaphor? The story of Jacob's dream is an important source for this tradition. It emphasizes the nearness of God, the ability to access God in moments of vulnerability and transition. It also speaks to an experience of wonder, of opening our eyes and saying, "Wow! How awesome is this Place!" For the rabbis of the

Mishnah, *HaMakom* was a name for God that implied a sense of God's nearness and love. They used the name *Hamakom* when they were talking about seeking compassion for themselves or others, when they gave a blessing of comfort to someone who was suffering, and when talking about how people should relate to one another.

What is a "place"? It is a physical space in which we experience ourselves in relation to that which is around us. Certain spaces make us feel contained and supported; they provide a structure within which we experience a sense of protection or refuge. Other spaces can make us feel our own smallness and give us a sense of wonder at the vastness that surrounds. A sacred "place" can be one especially designated for worship or meditation—a synagogue or mosque, a church or temple—or a place in nature, by the ocean or on a mountaintop. It might be a place where, like Jacob, we had a memorable, holy experience.

But the most important thing about "place" is that we're always in one. The underlying irony of calling God "*HaMakom* / The Place" is that there isn't just one place to encounter godliness—that can happen in *any* place. "Place" is here in this moment, right where we are. The metaphor of God as Place invites us to open ourselves to the potential godliness of any and every moment, in any place that we might find ourselves.

How Awesome Is This Place

When Jacob awakens from his dream, he exclaims, "*Mah norah haMakom hazeh*—How awesome is this Place!"[3] This nondescript rocky spot in the desert has suddenly become, in Jacob's mind, a "gateway to heaven." The emphasis in Jacob's exclamation isn't just on "*haMakom*/Place" but also on the word *hazeh*—"*this.*" If *Makom* is a name for an experience of godliness that we can access in any place, then by saying "how awesome is *this Makom,*" we acknowledge the potential for having this kind of expanded awareness in any moment, in any situation. It is *this* place, this spot that I am inhabiting in this moment, that holds the potential for direct experience of something sacred.

Interestingly, Jacob does not seem delighted by this realization. The text says quite explicitly that he is afraid—full of awe, but also a bit of trembling—when he realizes that "there is YHVH in this place." This is important. Too often I find that people associate "spiritual" with "pleasant." They assume that all spiritual experiences share a positive vibe, consisting either of ecstatic joy or blissful serenity (which is why too many people assume that they must not be "spiritual," since most of us don't feel bliss all that often). But as I mentioned earlier, Jacob is in quite a difficult emotional place when he has his dream. He is vulnerable and alone, and he doesn't seem entirely reassured even after he receives God's wonderful promises. Upon waking from his dream, Jacob is still fearful and mistrustful. Yet he realizes that he is in the presence of Something godly and powerful. He learns that there is godliness even in places where we wish we didn't have to be.

Sometimes we experience the sacred in moments of joy—at the birth of a baby, when making love or making music. And sometimes it happens at moments of sorrow and heartbreak, when we are broken open. Sometimes we experience it when we least expect it. To live in the reality of "how awesome is this Place" is to live our lives open to the possibility that there is a spark of the holy—a bit of wisdom, a deeper understanding, a sense of connection— available to us in any place, in any moment, even the most difficult. As Jacob realized, "There is YHVH in *this* place." Not just in the good or the perfect, but in the truth of what is.

The nineteenth-century Hasidic rabbi Aaron Perlow of Karlin commented on the Jacob story that each of us needs to find our special *makom,* a space in which we can nourish our spirits and fulfill whatever it is that we have been put on this planet to do. But he then goes on to say that each of us needs to do this "so that your heart not be in contention with the Place/*Hamakom*."[4] To "be in contention with the Place" suggests engaging in a fantasy that the truth of the present moment can be other than what it is. I can only be in one place—and this is it. Our spiritual challenge, according to Rabbi Perlow, is to not be in contention with the truth of our lives as we encounter it "in this place," even if we might wish to be anywhere but here.

Hamakom and Comfort

Jewish tradition associates the divine name *Hamakom* with comfort and compassion. This may be because the Hebrew word for compassion comes from the root for *womb*, which is the first "place" we all find ourselves in.[5] In rabbinic tradition, enduring in Jewish practice today, we use the epithet *Hamakom* when we extend a blessing of comfort to a mourner: "May *Hamakom* comfort you among all the mourners of Zion." In a text I cited earlier, Rabbi Judah used *Hamakom* in his blessing for those who were sick. God as the Place seems a fitting metaphor for those times when we seek comfort and compassion. When we find ourselves vulnerable, sad or frightened, we can imagine ourselves in a familiar place, surrounded by whatever it is that makes us feel supported. We can think of God as a Place to which we retreat to find comfort and relief.

There is a beautiful moment in the book of Exodus when Moses is pleading with YHVH for a clear sign that God is with him. Moses begs, "Show me Your Presence!" In response, God says, "*Hinei, makom iti*—Here, [there is] a place with Me."[6] God is inviting Moses into a very intimate Place, a Place where godliness dwells. Instructions then follow for what is to come, and Moses is warned that he won't be able to have a direct, visual experience of YHVH. When the revelation finally arrives, there are no visual pyrotechnics, no burning bushes or trembling mountains. Instead, Moses hears a new name for God, a series of adjectives describing God as kind and compassionate, caring and patient, with the capacity for endless forgiveness.[7]

Hinei, Makom iti—here, in this Place, you will find compassion and loving-kindness and endless mercy. What is this Place? It exists right here, in me, in you. As we expand our own capacity for compassion—compassion for ourselves, compassion for others—we create a *Makom* of refuge that we carry within us at all times.

Caring for the Place

To experience divinity as "Place" is to understand the essential sacredness of the very place of our lives—this beautiful planet Earth. In this understanding, God is not Something far away and "other": It is right here, in the ground beneath our feet. We are commanded to preserve, not destroy, the sacred Place in which we find ourselves as earthly beings. At a time when we are finally awakening to the profound danger that human technological achievements have wrought on the climate, and as we realize the precariousness of life on this planet, it is time for us to have compassion on this holy Place. If we love this Place that we call our home, then we must stop destroying it.

God as Place Practice

May the Place/HaMakom Bring You Comfort

To foster a sense of the sacred in connection to Place, take a little time to connect to one or two physical places that are meaningful to you. I find that drawing is a good way to open up sometimes hidden parts of my brain. So get yourself some crayons and a big piece of plain paper, and sit for a moment, thinking of a place you have been that is important to you, that carries positive associations. It might be a place that you visited once, or somewhere you find yourself on a regular basis. And it doesn't matter if you don't think you can draw! The intention here is to represent that place as best as you can. Think about the details that make this place special, and how it makes you feel when you're there.

If drawing is not your preference, you can do something similar as a writing exercise. Conjure up the place in your mind and begin writing with the phrase "I remember . . ." Write down everything you can remember about this place, writing freely without pause. When you come to a stopping point, you can start again with "I remember," and see what else comes. Fill in as many details as you remember, both about the place itself and your experience in it. You might hold on to your drawing or description, or recycle it once you're done; the main point of this exercise is to bring to your awareness your own special Place.

This can become your personal refuge, the *Makom* to which you turn in moments of loss or fear, anxiety or sadness. In those moments, bring this special place to mind, remembering how you felt, how you feel, when you are there. Invite your fear or sadness or anxiety into that place, knowing that it will be graciously received. Let The Place/ *HaMakom* hold the feelings, hold you.

Hinei Makom Iti / *Here, a Place with Me*

When Moses asks to see God's Presence, he is in the midst of trying to repair a significant breach in the relationship between God and the Israelite people, a breach caused by the creation of the golden calf (see chapter 32 in the book of Exodus for that story). In this moment, Moses is seeking compassion for both himself and his people. In response, YHVH invites him into a "place" where he hears God's true name: "Compassion and Mercy, Patience and Loving-Kindness, Truth and Endless Forgiveness."

Sometimes I like to read Torah stories the way a therapist once told me to interpret dreams: to assume all of the characters are me. In this story, the Israelites are that part of me that screws up, that goes astray, the part I get angry at and frustrated with. Moses is my better nature, the part of me that realizes that continually berating myself isn't particularly productive. And YHVH is the Source of compassion that I can draw on, my own capacity for compassion to which I always have access. The "*Makom*" into which the Moses part of me is invited is this "place" of compassion.

What I have learned over the years is that, with practice, it is possible to increase my capacity for compassion and loving response. In the metaphor of *Makom,* it is possible to expand this space within myself, a Godly place of compassion and loving-kindness for myself and others. I like to imagine this space as my own heart.

Here is a compassion practice that you can try, using the language of *Makom,* based on the Buddhist practice of *metta* meditation:

Find a comfortable place to sit, and find a position in which you can be both relaxed and alert. Take a moment to settle into your chair or onto a cushion, and take a few gentle breaths. Let your eyes close. Bring your awareness to your breath, seeing if you can notice the sensation of breathing in, and the sensation of breathing out. Don't try to breathe in any particular way, and stay relaxed. Imagine yourself breathing through the heart-space in your chest. Imagine that this space is gently expanding, becoming open and spacious.

As you sit and notice your breath, you can repeat this phrase to yourself, either in Hebrew or English:

Hinei makom iti (hee-NAY mah-COMB ee-TEE)
Here, a Place with me

Let yourself be gently drawn into this relaxed sense of spaciousness that you are creating. When the mind wanders, you can use the phrase to draw your attention back to the breath.

After about five minutes, you are invited to silently say these phrases of blessing. There may be thoughts or reactions that arise in response to the words; you can just notice these and let them go. There is no particular way you are supposed to feel as you say the words; the main thing is to mindfully repeat them, ideally for about five minutes for each set. Begin by sending these blessings to yourself:

May I be blessed with well-being.
May I be blessed with safety and protection.
May I be blessed with peace.

Repeat these phrases with the intention of wishing yourself well. After a few minutes, you are invited to bring someone to mind to whom you'd like to send these blessings. You might want to start with someone with whom you have a positive, relatively uncomplicated relationship. You can bring the person's face to mind. Silently say the same phrases, but with *you* instead of *I*:

May you be blessed with well-being.
May you be blessed with safety and protection.
May you be blessed with peace.

You may want to extend this practice to other people in your life, including those for whom you don't have such positive feelings. I would recommend building up to that, and not choosing the most difficult person in your life until you've done this practice for a little while. The point of the practice is not to magically make anyone's life better; it is simply to expand the capacity of your own heart and mind to feel compassion for yourself and others. It might not feel like much of anything is happening the first few times you do it, but over time, it is quite a powerful practice.

Close the practice by coming back to the breath, and back to the phrase *Hinei Makom iti* / Here, a Place with me.

Mah Norah Hamakom Hazeh / *How Awesome Is This Place*

Walking Meditation: Here is another type of meditation, to awaken the awareness of "this place." Find a space, either indoors or outdoors, where you can walk about ten or fifteen paces, back and forth. As you take each step, bring your awareness to the physical sensation of walking. You can notice the sensations in each leg as it lifts and extends, the sensations in the heel and ball of each foot. You might focus your awareness very narrowly on the bottom of the foot, or hold a more expansive awareness of your whole body as it moves through space. If the mind is wandering, a more focused attention for a few minutes can help settle your awareness back into the walking. You might notice sounds or sights.

The only "goal" here is to be present in this moment, in this place, noticing what there is to notice. Your mind, if it's at all like mine, will have lots of things it wants to do—memories to peruse, plans to make, stories to tell. You can gently notice all of that, and then bring your attention back to *this* place, *Hamakom hazeh.*

You can also use the phrase to redirect your attention: *Mah norah Hamakom hazeh* / How awesome is this Place. Take anywhere between ten to thirty minutes for this practice, walking back and forth, mindfully, gently, with awareness of "this place" that you find yourself in.

Do Not Be in Contention with Hamakom

For this practice, you'll need to make a little card with this phrase on it:

Mah norah Hamakom hazeh
How awesome is this place

Take the card (or cards, if you'd like to do this in a few places) and put it somewhere you don't associate with particularly positive or "spiritual" experiences: your car dashboard, your work computer or desk. When you're having a difficult or unpleasant moment in that space, let the card be a reminder: there is godliness in *this* place! You might want to say the phrase out loud, in Hebrew or English (the Hebrew is pronounced this way: MA nor-RAH hah-mah-COMB hah-ZEH). You can also keep a card in your pocket or purse and pull it out in difficult moments. Breathe. Read or recite the words on the card. Smile.

IF YOU TRULY LISTEN

In the spring of 1979, I attended an Elvis Costello concert in Washington, D.C.—one of the most religious experiences of my then young life. I was a junior in high school, and Elvis was my god. The concert was amazing. Costello wouldn't play unless everyone was standing up, and so we all were, atop the seats of our chairs, for the entire ninety minutes. The music went on without interruption or between-songs chatter; just one loud, raucous song after another, the audience singing along at the top of our lungs. At one point, I had to go out to the bathroom; when I stepped down from my chair, the sound became an undifferentiated roar. It was an all-encompassing ecstatic experience, and I can still feel a few of the tremors in my body today, many decades later.

What is it about a good rock concert that makes such

an indelible impression on us when we are young (or even when not so young)? It would be hard for me to tease out one element. I loved Costello's lyrics, and the sound of his voice, and how he stood, not moving, on the stage, daring us to love him in all his nerdy, antisocial glory. There were no pyrotechnics, no fancy lights or snazzy dancers. Just the music, the musicians, and us, the audience. A communication was happening that was somehow more than just the sum of its fairly simple parts.

In Jewish tradition, the peak religious experience in the Torah happens when the Israelites, newly freed from slavery in Egypt, arrive at Mount Sinai. There, they experience the mythical equivalent of a full-scale rock concert:

> *Now, it was on the third day, at daybreak: there were thunder-sounds, and lightning, a heavy cloud on the mountain and an exceedingly strong sound of the ram's horn . . . Now Mount Sinai smoked all over, since YHVH had come down upon it in fire; its smoke went up like the smoke of a furnace, and all of the mountain trembled exceedingly.*[1]

Talk about pyrotechnics! Fire and smoke, thunder and lightning, the loud sound of horns. And, in the midst of all this, a singular communication:

Now the ram's horn sound was growing exceedingly stronger—Moses was speaking, and God answered him in a voice . . . God spoke all these words, saying . . .[2]

What follows is what later came to be called the Ten Commandments. In Jewish tradition, the entire Torah was received that day: both the first five books of the Bible, and the entire chain of rabbinic tradition, the commentary on those books. For the early rabbis, what happened at Mount Sinai was a spiritual Big Bang, the reverberations of which continue to the present day.

While there is a lot of imagery at play in the various biblical depictions of Sinai, what stands out is the experience of *sound*—in Hebrew, *kol*. In the Exodus account in chapter 19, this word—*kol*—repeats four times in three verses. In the translation I offered above, it appears in English as "thunder-sounds," "sound of the ram's horn," and God's "voice." When Moses retells the story of Sinai in the book of Deuteronomy, the word *kol* features prominently again, appearing seven times in the space of six verses.[3]

Those of us who are familiar with the Hebrew Bible may not think much of this emphasis on God's "voice," considering it just another aspect of God as Big Person, the Ruler who speaks. After all, God talks quite a bit in the early books of the Bible! But deeper exploration reveals that Voice does not necessarily depend on a Speaker. The experience of voice, of sound, was a fundamental way that our ancestors experienced the divine—sometimes with words, and sometimes not.[4]

In the Beginning

The authors of the Torah imagined the Creative Power of the universe as a Voice speaking each aspect of Creation into being. In the very first chapter of Genesis, God says, over and over again, "Let there be," and there was—light and dark, seas and heaven and earth, plants and animals, and finally, human beings.

It is in the story of these first humans, Adam and Eve, that we get the first appearance of the word *kol* in the Torah. Defying the one *don't* that God has given them, Eve and then Adam eat the fruit of the forbidden Tree of Knowledge of Good and Evil. When a new kind of awareness dawns on them, they hide from God. And then: "*They heard the* kol *of YHVH God walking around in the Garden, at the breezy time of day.*"[5]

It is somewhat odd that an apparently disembodied voice is taking a walk in the Garden! Perhaps the Torah is trying to get us to pay attention to the power of this Voice, and the question It asks: "Where are you?"[6]

This is God's first question to humans, and the first question asked in the entire Bible. "Where are you?" seems to have less to do with a literal inquiry into Adam and Eve's location (surely YHVH can figure that out) and more about taking responsibility for their actions. "Why are you hiding?" the Voice seems to be saying. In response to the next question—"Did you eat of the tree from which you were told not to?"—Adam and Eve both duck responsibility. Adam blames Eve, and Eve blames the snake. Having exercised their God-given ability to make choices, the first humans learn the consequences of eating from the forbidden tree. They will become mortal beings, experiencing the pain of childbirth and the difficulty of physical labor, and will have to leave the Garden of Eden forever. They have become "like God" in their ability to know good and evil—and in their power to use their own voices for bad or for good.

The human capacity for evil manifests in short order when Adam and Eve's son Cain murders their other son, Abel. In this strange little story, we find God's next question—this time directed at Cain: "Where is your brother, Abel?"[7] Like his parents in the Garden, Cain doesn't immediately take responsibility for what he has done. God's response includes this fascinating use of the word *kol:* "What have you done? The voice of your brother's blood cries out to Me from the ground!"[8]

So what do these early Torah stories tell us about the power of *kol*? They suggest that the metaphor of Voice encompasses Creation, the mysteries of life and death, and the relationship of humans and the divine. The power of *kol* is wielded both by God and by human beings, and seems closely linked to the ability to discern right from wrong.

Seeing the Sounds

In his book *How to Be Heard: Secrets for Powerful Listening and Speaking,* sound expert Julian Treasure notes that "the human body is 70 percent water, which makes us rather good conductors of sound. It's not surprising, then, that sound can powerfully affect us physiologically, changing our heart rate, breathing, hormone secretions and even our brain waves. All our bodily rhythms can be affected by sound."[9] Perhaps the divine *kol* of the early chapters of Genesis reflects this foundational effect of sound waves upon us. We humans are conductors of the godly Voice.

Sound is foundational to human experience whether or not we have the physical ability to hear. In the words of

Evelyn Glennie, a virtuoso percussionist who is profoundly deaf: "Hearing is basically a specialized form of touch. Sound is simply vibrating air which the ear picks up and converts to electrical signals, which are then interpreted by the brain. The sense of hearing is not the only sense that can do this, touch can do this too . . . For some reason we tend to make a distinction between hearing a sound and feeling a vibration, in reality they are the same thing."[10]

My colleague Rabbi Darby Leigh, who is also profoundly deaf, connects this insight to the verse in the book of Exodus immediately following God's instructions to the Israelites: "*All of the people saw the voices* [kolot], *and the lightning, and the sound* [kol] *of the ram's horn, and the mountain smoking.*"[11] What does it mean to say that "the people *saw* the voices"? The Torah seems to be conveying an experience of sound that goes beyond our usual sense of hearing. In our conversation about this text, Darby told me that as a deaf person, he can see himself present at Sinai because "everyone *saw* the voices." Given his experience of needing to see a person when they speak, whether he is reading their lips or watching them as they sign, "seeing" and "listening" are intimately connected. Darby says that he would translate *kol* as "vibration." In our conversation, we connected this translation to contemporary physics and string theory—the idea that everything in the universe is vibrating. Darby told me: "We are saturated by these vibrational waves . . . God is the Vibration that saturates the universe."

When we understand God through the metaphor of Voice, we are giving expression to a foundational experience of Something moving through us, Something that both shapes who we are and allows us to express ourselves. Voice is about communication and connection, what we put out into the universe and what we take in.

Each According to Their Strength

In a wonderful rabbinic commentary on God speaking at Sinai, the early rabbis taught that every Israelite received the divine Voice "according to their strength."[12] Whatever their age or gender or experience, each person received the Voice according to their personal ability or capacity. This teaching suggests that the Voice at Sinai could have overwhelmed those who experienced It—yet this did not happen. Each person was able to channel what they needed to receive in such a way that the Voice became life-sustaining instead of life-threatening.

I love this image of that which was spoken at Sinai—spiritual teachings, instructions for living, cosmic revelation—

IF YOU TRULY LISTEN

being heard in hundreds of thousands of unique ways. Each person present received what they needed to hear in that moment. By implication, those of us who continue to listen for the Voice similarly receive it "according to our strength."

Too often we are told that religion means uniformity of thought and practice, that "God's word" is eternal, unchanging, and uncompromisingly rigid. Yet this rabbinic tradition makes clear that speaking and listening is an interactive process that depends as much on the listener as the speaker. What we are able to hear depends on how well we listen, and on what we need to receive in any particular moment. According to the Hasidic teacher Rabbi Menachem Mendel of Vorki, when the Torah says that the Israelites "saw the voices" at Sinai, this means "that they saw and realized that one must take the Voice into oneself and make it one's own."[13]

When I was thirty years old, I entered rabbinical school. A question I've heard a lot in the intervening years is, "What made you decide to become a rabbi?" My answer is usually, "I don't know." Becoming a rabbi wasn't something I thought about as a young person (when being female would have disqualified me in any case), and I didn't arrive at the decision by any well-thought-out logical process, or in a mystical moment of a "call." As I've told my story over the years, I've come to realize that this particular decision was the result of an accumulation of moments of hearing many different voices. These moments included:

- A friend of the family wondering about my administrative job in a nonprofit when I was in my late twenties, surprised because she thought I "wasn't good at" what I was doing (I actually was, but what she meant was, "You're a creative person who used to write musicals in high school, what happened to all that?").
- A man selling me something at a Jewish crafts fair who asked me if I went to the Reconstructionist Rabbinical College (I answered, "Not yet!").
- Performing a few Jewish songs at a national gathering of community organizers, after which one of the women told me that I "had a gift"— which I took to mean that if I had a gift, I had a responsibility to use it for the greater good in some way.
- Listening to a speech by the Reverend Martin Luther King Jr. on my car radio one day, and realizing that if I was going to do social justice work, then this was the language I wanted to be using—a language grounded in moral vision and God's spirit.

All of these moments—and probably many more—ultimately coalesced into my decision to explore a career in the rabbinate. The decision that would shape my adult life was the result of a process of discernment that I didn't even realize I was engaged in: an ongoing process of listening.

It is perhaps no coincidence that the key prayer in Jewish tradition is a section of Torah that lifts up the instruction to "listen":

Listen, Israel, YHVH our God, YHVH is One. And you shall love YHVH your God with all your heart, and with all your soul, and with all that you have. Take these words which I command today to heart, and teach them to your children, and speak them when you sit in your house and when you walk along the road, when you lie down and when you rise.[14]

We call this prayer the *Shema*—after the first word, which means "listen." These verses about "listening" are from the book of Deuteronomy, in which the command to hear and to do is repeated over and over again. In the Torah, listening to the divine Voice is connected to *action*. To truly listen to God's Voice is to have something demanded of us. If we can listen with an open heart and mind—to the people we encounter in our daily lives; to the beauty of the

natural world; to our own experience—we have the opportunity to discern what is being asked of us in each moment.

Crying Out

In May 2003, I was teaching a class on death and dying in
Jewish tradition when I got a message that Gina, my spouse,
was trying to reach me. She wanted me to come home as
soon as the class ended. When I got back to the house,
she sat me down and said, "Bill is gone." And that is how I
learned that my sixty-four-year-old father was dead.

The news was a complete and total shock. Since his
first heart attack a quarter century earlier, my dad had lived
a pretty healthy life. He'd stopped smoking, he exercised
and ate well, he knew how to relax and enjoy himself. In
fact, he'd gone fishing the day before he died; we have
a beautiful picture of him holding up a big fish he'd just
caught on his friend's boat. And then, the next day, while
he was out biking with one of his oldest friends, he suffered
a massive heart attack and died almost instantly.

That May evening, after calling my mother and brother
and booking a flight home to D.C., I took a walk. It was late,
and our suburban neighborhood was dark and quiet. As I
walked, I cried and I shouted, my voice disappearing into

the night. I don't remember my thoughts or, if I prayed, what the words of that prayer might have been. But I remember my cries, as if my broken and shocked heart were speaking its own wordless language of grief.

I also remember having a sense that somehow God was present in this. Reflecting back on that moment, I wonder if I was connecting to *kol,* to Voice, via my own inarticulate cry. In crying out, I felt a little less alone.

The Hebrew Bible is filled with stories not just of the divine Voice reaching human beings but of human voices reaching God. As the biblical scholar James Kugel notes, it is a particular kind of communication that YHVH "hears": the cry of the suffering and the oppressed.[15] In the book of Exodus, as the Israelites suffer in their bondage to Pharaoh, we read: "*The children of Israel groaned from the slavery, and they cried out, and their cry rose up to God. God heard their moaning, and God remembered the covenant with Abraham, Isaac, and Jacob. God saw the children of Israel, and God knew.*"[16] What is noticeable about this passage is that it doesn't say that the Israelites cried out *to* God; rather, they simply called out, and were heard. The agonized cry of the enslaved Israelites causes YHVH to become aware and to act, setting in motion the Exodus from Egypt.

In the metaphor of Voice, how might we understand this idea of our heartfelt human voices reaching God? What does it mean to say, in the words of the Psalms, that "*those who cry out, YHVH hears, and saves them from all their troubles; YHVH is near to the broken-hearted, and brings liberation to those whose spirits are crushed*"?[17]

There is an interesting commentary about the Israelites calling out from their bondage that helps me understand the power of the anguished cry. On the face of it, it doesn't entirely make sense that only when the groans of the Israelites "rose up to God" did YHVH finally become aware of what was going on. Did God really forget all about the covenant with Abraham and his descendants, and not care what was happening to the children of Israel?

The great Hasidic master Yehudah Leib of Ger understands this passage as describing not so much what was going on with God but what was going on with the enslaved Israelites: "Before this, they were so deep in exile that they did not even feel they were in exile. Now that they understood exile and groaned, a little redemption began."[18]

For Rabbi Yehudah Leib, crying out is the first step in a process of transformation. We cannot change our situation until we are aware that we are suffering and give voice to that suffering. Sometimes we become so used to our condition, we don't even realize how bad off we are. Or perhaps we feel our pain, but keep it to ourselves. When we give voice to our suffering, we have the opportunity to shift our own awareness, and the awareness of others.

The great sixteenth-century rabbi Judah Loew of Prague said the power of *kol* is that it comes from the innermost part of a person.[19] Giving voice to pain often means giving voice to what is most true for us. No oppressive situation in this world has ever changed until the people most affected speak out, voicing their sorrow and their anger. When the Israelites received the commandments at Mount Sinai, God told them: *"You shall not oppress any widow or orphan; if you do mistreat them, they will surely cry out to Me, and I will hear their cry . . . For I am compassionate."*[20] It is the cry of the most vulnerable in a society that activates the Source of Compassion and the Power of Liberation. Listening to the pain of those who have been demeaned and marginalized is one way that we can hear the Voice that spoke at Sinai, the call to build a better world.

Song and Silence

There are two elements found in every spiritual and religious tradition that resonate with the power of Voice: music, and the sound of silence. Each of these modalities offer opportunities for transformative spiritual experience.

Dr. Bernice Johnson Reagon, the renowned scholar, activist, and musician, shared this beautiful insight into the power of singing in the Black church in a 1991 interview with Bill Moyers:

> Songs are a way to get to singing. The singing is what you're aiming for and the singing is running this sound through your body. You cannot sing a song and not change your condition . . . My temperature—I'm a little flushed and I open my mouth and I do one of these songs and my whole something is different. And I can just feel it . . . There are some people who come to church and they try their best to leave the way they came. But the reason you leave your house to go to church is to go through this exercise and I am talking about a culture that thinks it is important to exercise this part of your being. The part of your being that is tampered with when you run this sound through your body is a part of you that our culture thinks should be developed and cultivated, that you should be familiar with, that you should be able to get to as often as possible and that if it's not developed, you are underdeveloped as a human being. If you go through your life and you don't meet this part of yourself, somehow the culture has failed you.[21]

In her reflections on the practice of sacred chant, Rabbi Shefa Gold notes that "when I chant, I am communicating with and awakening places inside me that need to hear and be touched by the chant."[22] Both Dr. Reagon and Rabbi Gold point us to the deeper power of *kol* that manifests as song. We don't merely sing in order to make a beautiful sound but to develop and express something deep within us. And we sing to connect with others. I have heard many times from my congregants over the years that while they don't always understand the Hebrew words of our prayer book, they feel a sense of spiritual connection when we sing those words together. There is power in the joining together of voices, finding harmony in the recitation of ancient texts, beyond the literal meaning of the words.

From the soaring voices of the Mormon Tabernacle Choir to the sacred chant of Sufi Muslims and Tibetan monks to Native American ritual drumming, it is hard to imagine spiritual practice without music. Every religion utilizes song in some way. Similarly, there is no sacred tradition that does not incorporate the practice of silence. Too often we think of silence as the absence of sound, rather than—like music—as a type of sound, a manifestation of *kol*. In the documentary *Touch the Sound*,[23] Evelyn Glennie says, "Silence is probably one of the loudest sounds, and one of the heaviest sounds that you're ever likely to experience." Julian Treasure builds on this insight, writing: "Silence is not only a sound: it is the context for all sound. Without the gaps, words and musical notes would be a meaningless jumble."[24]

In a wonderful story about the prophet Elijah in the biblical book of Kings, the prophet retraces Moses's steps to Mount Sinai, where he hopes to have an experience of God. At first, he seems to be getting the full pyrotechnic performance that the Israelites experienced in the book of Exodus. He goes out on the mountain, *"and here, YHVH passes by, and a great and mighty wind, splitting mountains and shattering stones"* but *"YHVH is not in the wind."* And after the wind, there is *"a great quaking; and YHVH is not in the quaking."* And then comes fire, *"and YHVH is not in the fire."* And finally, after the fire, a *kol d'mama daka*—which can be translated as "a thin, silent voice" or perhaps "a sound of soft silence."[25] Unlike the thunderous Voice that reached Moses and the Israelites, Elijah discovers God in the *kol* of silence.

I have a practice of going every year on a weeklong silent meditation retreat. When I try to describe this experience to others, most people get stuck on the idea of not being able to talk for seven days. But "silence" in this context means much more that; it is a process of learning to pay attention to what is happening in my body, mind, and heart from moment to moment. This practice of silence includes refraining not just from conversation but also from reading and writing, all in the service of being fully present to whatever is arising right now. There is plenty to listen to: the instructions from the meditation teachers; the clang of cutlery during meals; the sounds of birds and passing cars; even my own breathing. Most revealing is the inner chatter of my mind. In the silence, I start to notice how loud things are in my head almost all of the time!

If music is a powerful way to connect with others, then silence is an indispensable mechanism for connecting with oneself. I only half jokingly tell people that one good silent retreat is worth at least two years of therapy. Once the daily noise is turned off—the noise of the news, of conversation, of a million distractions coming at us from our screens—we can find some space to listen to what is going on inside of us. I wouldn't say it's an easy practice, but it has brought me an enormous amount over the past twenty years: insight, a greater capacity for patience and compassion, and some profound moments of both heartbreak and joy. In the silence, I am able to hear the Voice that, according to rabbinic tradition, calls out every day from Sinai: the ongoing communication of sacred instructions for living. In the silence, I can become a more open, mindful vessel for the godly vibrations that fill the universe.

God as Voice Practice

In the Song of Songs, the biblical book of erotic love poems that can be read as a conversation between God and the spiritual seeker, we find this beautiful verse: *I sleep, but my heart wakes; the voice of my beloved knocks!*[26] Attuning to the "voice of the Beloved"—the divine Voice—is a process of waking up. To awaken to the power of *kol* is to pay attention to the world around us, and to activate our own voice, our own deepest yearnings and aspirations. The following practices are intended to foster our capacity to both speak and listen in ways that will wake us up to the truths of our own lives.

Hitbodedut/Talking Practice: Before the invention of talk therapy, a famous Hasidic master of the eighteenth century, Rebbe Nachman of Bratslav, recommended a practice known as *hitbodedut* (which can be translated as "being alone with yourself"). Rebbe Nachman would go out into the forest every day for a set amount of time and speak aloud to God. He encouraged his students to use this practice to ask for what they needed, to draw closer to a sense of God's presence, and to understand how they were each meant to do their particular service in the world. It was a time to break open one's heart, and to speak from the deepest place within.

In the metaphor of Voice, we can understand *hitbodedut* as an opportunity to use our own voices to connect to Something both within and beyond us. Rabbi David Jaffe describes this practice as "speaking one's desire" and in so doing, "turning what we deeply care about and yearn for into a prayer." What is important is that we engage in it as a conversation, whatever our beliefs about Who or What may (or may not) be listening. As Rabbi Jaffe writes: "I've had students talk with their 'higher wisdom' or 'ideal support' . . . Conversations can begin, 'I don't know who I am talking to, and this feels really awkward, but here I go.' If you wish you could relate to God but feel blocked, you can say that as well: 'God, I have no idea if you exist, but I really wish I could sense you.' You can even talk to yourself. Anything goes in this practice of speaking one's desire, and you get to start exactly where you are with no pretense."[27]

To do this practice:

- Find a place where you will not feel strange talking out loud (and/or crying, shouting, singing). Rebbe Nachman suggested going out into nature, but any space that feels good to you is fine.
- Begin talking to God / the Universe—to Something "out there," regardless of whether or not you think you are being heard. You might imagine your words

reaching the Source of Compassion. Just pretend if you need to, but use the language of "you."

- Talk about whatever you like; share what's in your heart. You might ask a question you are wrestling with, or talk about what you really want in your life right now. You can express gratitude or sorrow; you can notice what is in front of you or repeat a verse from a sacred text or poem that moves you. The main thing is that you don't stop talking.

- Make a set time for your *hitbodedut*—ten to fifteen minutes is good, more if you can! Even if you can't think of what to say, just keep talking. It's fine to repeat one word over and over. When your time is up, sit quietly for a few minutes, and see what rises up in the silence; notice the echoes in your heart or mind.

Like any practice, *hitbodedut* takes on power if done regularly. Try making a set time each day for a week.

The Wagon-Driver Moment—a Listening Practice: There is a wonderful story told about another eighteenth-century Hasidic rabbi, Moshe Leib of Sassov. While walking along the road one day, he was asked by a wagon driver to pick up something that had fallen from the wagon. When Rabbi Moshe Leib responded that he wasn't able to, the wagon driver replied, "You are able to, you just don't want to."

In this moment, Moshe Leib heard the word of God speaking directly to him: "You are able to, you just don't want to."

I love the idea that an esteemed rabbi would hear—in the rebuke of a somewhat obnoxious wagon driver—a personal message from God. A later rabbi commented on this story: "Whatever transpires during the course of our lives, whatever we see or hear, is all the voice of God speaking to us . . . We must always be listening to hear God's voice speaking to us."[28] In experiencing the divine as Voice, we can attune ourselves to what the world is telling us in even the most mundane interactions.

Choose a day, and set an intention to be listening, all day long, as if God / Voice / the Universe is communicating directly with you. What do you need to hear today? What messages do you receive? You might pay attention to actions you do every day, or to interactions with other people. What do you learn about yourself when you pay attention in this way? What do others have to teach you?

This listening practice is different from "having an opinion" about things you observe. Instead of your habitual reactions, try to bring an element of surprise to what you encounter. Be brave, like Rabbi Moshe Leib, and see if you can find a divine message, intended just for you, in a challenging situation. This can be a great opportunity to turn a situation that might lead to defensiveness or anger into a learning moment. Just do it gently, and with a sense of humor, if possible!

The Sound of Silence: The practice of mindfulness meditation is one I recommend to everyone, and it begins with developing the capacity to focus and quiet the mind. These days, you can access mindfulness instructions via a multitude of apps and websites. If you live in an area with a mindfulness meditation center, I highly recommend you check it out. You don't have to go on a weeklong retreat to enjoy the benefits of this practice (although it's a powerful experience if you can do it). You'll just need to find a place to sit that is relatively quiet, and a willingness to shut everything off for ten to twenty (or more) minutes each day. I particularly recommend a practice called *insight meditation* (also known as *Vipassana* in Buddhist circles), which teaches both how to quiet the mind and how to become aware of our habits of mind. Here is a beginning instruction:

Find a comfortable yet alert sitting position (on a chair is fine, with your feet on the ground and your hands either resting on your legs or in your lap). Close your eyes, and bring your attention to your body. Notice what it feels like to sit. You can notice where your body touches the chair or the floor; notice where your hands are touching your body.

One helpful technique is to bring your attention to the sensation of breath: notice breathing in, and breathing out. These instructions to pay attention to the body are a basic concentration practice, intended to settle the mind. It is in the nature of the mind for your thoughts to flit all over the place; that is completely normal. What you want to do is find an "anchor," a physical sensation, that you can return to when your attention wanders. You can use the sensation of breathing, or of your feet on the ground, or your hands resting in your lap. Simply choose one physical "anchor," and then set an intention to be present to and aware of that sensation, from moment to moment.

You are *not* a "bad meditator" when your attention wanders—you are simply human and alive! The "insight" happens when you realize that your attention has wandered. In that moment, you can gently bring your awareness back to the body, back to the breath. Try doing this for ten minutes every morning (set a timer, so you don't have to worry about knowing when to stop). The goal is simple, if not easy: to be aware of what is happening in your body and in your mind, moment to moment. The tendency of our minds is to spend very little time in the present moment. We're usually digging around in the past, or imagining the future, or off in a fantasy. Our minds are like restless puppies, endlessly bounding around from here to there. We use the body as an anchor because, unlike our minds, it has no choice; it is always right here.

During one ten-minute sit, you might have one or two minutes of awareness; in another, you might have ten seconds. Be gentle with yourself, and remember that even the intention to sit and be mindful is beneficial. Once you are able to sit and have some awareness of the present moment, you can begin to notice other things: whether the physical or emotional sensations you are feeling are pleasant, or unpleasant, or neutral; how your mind reacts to certain sensations; where your thoughts tend to go. This is what is meant by "insight."

The Voice that speaks through this practice is that of wisdom, helping us better understand ourselves. It helps us discover the freedom that comes from being able to sit with whatever arises in our minds and hearts. To learn more about mindfulness meditation, you can check out books by Thich Nhat Hanh, Sharon Salzberg, Joseph Goldstein, Jack Kornfield, Christina Feldman, Sylvia Boorstein, Pema Chödrön, and many others.

Sacred Chant: Joey Weisenberg, a wonderful musician and Jewish prayer leader, writes that "melodies form a divine ladder that connects the Earth with the heavens . . . When we sing, we hope to allow ourselves to experience a state of elevation, a taste of the heavens, a glimpse of the best version of ourselves."[29] Whether or not we think we "have a good voice," singing is a potentially transformational experience. As we sing or chant, we become vessels for the Voice that speaks through each one of us.

In chapter 3, I shared some practice instructions from Rabbi Shefa Gold, who has done pioneering work in the realm of Jewish sacred chant, using verses from the Hebrew Bible and Jewish liturgy. I highly recommend her book *The Magic of Hebrew Chant* to learn more about this practice, and to see music for many of the chants she has composed (which you can also hear on her website, rabbishefagold .com). Depending on your background, you might like to explore other sacred chant and song traditions, which include Gregorian chant and gospel in the Christian tradition, *dhikr* (*zikr*) in Islam, and Hindu and Buddhist chants, among many others. All involve the repetitive singing of sacred phrases, and it is the chanting that helps bring the text deeper into our minds and hearts. Repetition gives sacred chant its power, so its best if you can set some period of time—ideally at least twenty minutes—to practice.

Niggun / Song from the Heart: Hasidic Judaism, a spiritual movement that swept across the Eastern European Jewish community beginning in the eighteenth century, features a kind of sacred song called *niggun,* or wordless melody. These tunes can be joyous or heartrending, and are meant to express the deepest yearnings of the heart. Rabbi Kalonymus Kalman Shapira, also known as the Piezetzner Rebbe, who perished in the Warsaw ghetto during the Holocaust, taught this practice to his students:

Find a phrase from a *niggun* you know and sit facing a wall, or just close your eyes. Imagine that you are coming to pour out your soul to God, with song and melody which come from the innermost part of your heart. Then you will certainly feel that your soul is coming out as you sing. If at first you were singing slowly before your soul in order to arouse it from its sleep, slowly, slowly you will feel that your soul has begun to sing on its own . . .

It will happen sometimes that as you sing, without intending it, you will spontaneously begin to speak words of prayer . . . It also happens sometimes that you will not be aroused to speak words of prayer, and you will not feel any need to ask for something from God; nevertheless, you will feel something hard to describe, a kind of throwing yourself at God to endear yourself to [God], like a child who in a sweet way is pestering his parent—he does not want anything but is just moaning and sighing, "Daddy, Mommy" . . . For with regard to knowing how to bring out the soul there are many things to be learned from children, for a child's actions are without conscious intention, and her soul just naturally expresses itself through actions and gestures.

This is not only so with *niggunim* of the broken heart but also with melodies that express joy; you can use all of them for bringing out your soul . . . And you do not have to raise your voice either, for it is possible to sing in the merest whisper and have it heard in heaven.[30]

If you would like to try this practice, you can use a musical phrase from a traditional Hasidic *niggun* or from another sacred song, or see if a tune arises spontaneously as you begin to sing. The intention is to sing from your heart; you may need to trust that you have within you such a source of song! Rabbi Shapira instructs to sing in such a way that you awaken your soul from sleep. You might want to start singing gently, as if to your own soul, and then give yourself over to the repetition of the *niggun*. You can imagine that the divine Voice is singing through you, or that you are reaching out to the divine with your voice. Whether you sing loudly or softly, joyously or with a broken heart, keep singing, and give yourself over to wherever the *niggun* takes you.

6

· · · · ·

ROCK OF MY HEART

A Rock in a Weary Land

In the winter of 2017, I began visiting people being detained in a local prison for various immigration violations (and sometimes for no violation at all). I met a Guatemalan father of four who had been living and working in the U.S. for decades without any trouble; an elderly Iraqi man with serious health problems; lesbians from Uganda seeking asylum from the horrifying abuse they had experienced at home. None had done anything particularly wrong, yet they were stuck in this prison for months, often separated from their spouses and children, the threat of deportation hanging over them. Each person, each story, was different, but what struck me about so many of these people was their incredible faith in God. Separated from their families and community, having no idea how long they would be in this situation, they somehow held on. They had a palpable sense of God's presence with them, even—or especially—in their darkest moments. While I was ostensibly the religious figure in the visiting room, on more than one occasion I felt that the faith of the person sitting across from me far exceeded my own.

The image that came to me in those moments was of God as these people's rock, their refuge and strength. There are numerous biblical verses in which God is called *Rock,* and many seem as if they were written by people in circumstances similar to those I met in prison:

> *To you YHVH I cry: my Rock, do not be silent to me, for if you are silent to me, I will be like those who go down into the pit. . . . Save me quickly; be for me a Rock of refuge . . . For you are my Rock and my fortress . . . Be for me a sheltering Rock that I can always come to.*[1]

For the detainees I visited, God as "sheltering Rock" was a source of strength and resilience, a "fortress" protecting them from despair, a "Rock of refuge" during lonely and confusing times.

The biblical metaphor of God as Rock is associated with a time of fear and struggle in the early life of King David. Before he became king, the young David was forced to flee into the wilderness, pursued by a jealous and increasingly paranoid King Saul. He hid in caves and rocky places in the Judean desert for many months before finally emerging victorious. The Book of Samuel, which recounts David's long and complex life, includes a poem/prayer in David's voice, *"on the day that YHVH delivered him from the hand of all his enemies, and from the hand of Saul."* In this poem, David says:

> *YHVH is my Rock and my fortified place, a rescuer for me. My God is my Rock, I take refuge in It; my shield and the strength that saves me; my fortress and refuge; my savior, you save me from violence.*[2]

This poem also appears in the book of Psalms, and indeed many of the psalms that call on God as Rock are attributed to David. Perhaps there was a tradition associating David's experience of seeking shelter in the craggy cliffs of the Judean desert with the image of God as Rock. A personal experience of finding refuge gave shape to an enduring metaphor for divine shelter and protection. In turn, this metaphor has spoken to many others seeking safety from harm. The refrain of a powerful African American spiritual, rooted in the experience of slavery, draws directly on the biblical tradition of God as Rock:

My God is a rock in the weary land, weary land, in the
weary land
My God is a rock in the weary land
Shelter in the time of storm[3]

I first heard this sung by Bessie Jones of the Georgia Sea Island Singers, recorded in 1961.[4] Jones, born in 1902, most likely learned this song from her grandfather Jet Sampson, who as a child was kidnapped in Africa and brought to America as a slave. Sampson passed on to his granddaughter songs and other cultural traditions from his time on plantations in Virginia and Georgia.

I wonder what it must have been like for Bessie Jones to hear these words sung by a man who had survived slavery, who had experienced Emancipation and the promise of Reconstruction and then the violence and despair of Jim Crow. What must that image of God as a sheltering Rock have meant to Mr. Sampson, as he endured the oppression of slavery and its aftermath? What inspiration and hope did it give Ms. Jones and her contemporaries, as they added their voices to the struggle for African American civil rights in the 1950s and '60s?

The legacy of God as Rock is a powerful one. Whatever our own experiences of suffering, the metaphor of Rock offers the possibility of finding protection and shelter when we feel besieged and weak, a place of rest in the "weary land" of our lives. It attests to a Power that literally grounds us in the solidity of the earth. The "sheltering Rock that I can always come to" promises that in the turmoil and pain of this world, healing can be found.

Rock of My Heart

Many people I know are drawn to rocks, whether water-smoothed pebbles on the beach or polished stones in a shop. One of the most beautiful and unique gifts I received when I was ordained as a rabbi was a geode filled with bright blue crystals, which sits on my desk and reminds me that—as my friend wrote in her card—"at the core, we sparkle." Tucked into my closet is a box filled with stones and shells collected in my travels with Gina. Taking a tiny bit of earth away from a place I've visited always feels like a meaningful kind of connection.

Reflecting on the appeal of rocks, Patricia Adams Farmer writes that "the energy of rocks is particularly mysterious and primordial . . . [A rock] radiates a personality of some-thing strong and trustworthy—and forever present in the world, remaining long after we are gone. A rock is very sure of itself, of its past and its future. And it has reason to be. When we pick up a rock, we are not just holding a lump of minerals: we are holding a piece of eternity in our hands."[5]

One of the "rock names" of YHVH in the Bible, *Tzur Olamim,* captures this sense of eternity. It is sometimes translated "Rock of Ages," and can also be translated as "everlasting Rock" or "ancient Rock."[6] When I first visited the Judean desert as a teenager, I was deeply moved by the landscape, which is dominated by limestone mountains from the Late Cretaceous period, seventy to eighty million years old. I climbed one of the mountains near Ein Gedi, the area where King David took shelter, and found a rock outcropping that offered protection from the sun. Sitting beneath this rock, looking out at the Judean hills, I mused on what it must have been like to try to survive in such a harsh environment. The landscape felt paradoxically welcoming and challenging, all at the same time.

Viewing the layers upon layers of rock in a mountainside millions of years old, I felt the sense of vastness—in time and in space—that gives mountains their sacred quality. And I also experienced a deep sense of connection with the earth's history. In his commentary on the opening verse of Psalm 95, "*Let us sing to YHVH, make a joyful noise to the Rock of our liberation!*" Dr. Arthur Walker-Jones writes:

Like all planets, Earth grew when stardust coalesced into larger and larger bodies of Rock. Rock forms both Earth and mountains. Lava from volcanoes creates land. Soil erodes from Rock and allows for the growth of plants. Animals are made up of minerals from Earth, and rely on minerals from plants and other animals. Rock surrounds and cradles the sea. In brief, Psalm 95 identifies God with Earth and allows for an ecological understanding of the creator as part of creation, as God in Earth.[7]

The earth-centric understanding of God that Walker-Jones celebrates here also helps connect us to an earthy experience of the sacred. We, like all animals, are made up of minerals from the earth. "God in Earth" is also God in us. In Jewish tradition, God as Rock is often associated with a powerful *personal* experience of the divine. YHVH is called "my Rock," "Rock of my strength," "Rock of our lives," and "Rock of my heart."

I especially love this last epithet, *Tzur levavi,* "Rock of my heart." It comes from a verse in Psalm 73: "*My flesh and my heart fail; the Rock of my heart and my portion is God forever.*"[8] The teaching here is that alongside the limitations inherent in this human body and mind, there is Something else that will not fail me. "Rock of *my* heart" suggests that somewhere within myself I can access the qualities associated with Rock, the "personality of something strong and trustworthy" that Farmer describes. A nineteenth-century rabbi known as Malbim understood this verse to be referring to an aspect of divinity within each of us—the soul—which he calls "the rock upon which the integrity of our heart stands."[9] This inner Rock is our own true godly nature. As such, its capacity is vast and unending, as expansive as the Mojave Desert, and as beautiful.

Now, it is very possible that you are skeptical of such a claim. I admit that there are many days when the only stoniness I feel in my own heart is despair at the world, or anger at those doing all the damage. If God as "Rock in a weary land" promises some measure of refuge from the suffering of this world, how is the "Rock of my heart" related to the possibility of healing and protection?

When I hold a stone in my hand and contemplate its qualities, I see how time and pressure have combined to shape it. Some rocks are forged from fiery lava, others smoothed by flowing water or altered by shifts in the earth's crust. While we may think of rocks as inert, the reality is they change and metamorphose over time, in response to their surroundings. So too in our lives we go through stresses and pressures; we endure abrupt shifts in our circumstances and the fires of loss and disappointment. These experiences shape us into who we are. What I have found is that if I can be open to *all* of my experience, then great wisdom becomes accessible to me. In a beautiful essay on lessons learned from a boulder she passes by each day, Nita Gilger writes:

> Each crevice in the boulder and each wrinkle on my hands show the passage of time and life. If every crack in the rock and every line on my face could tell their stories, I know that the messages would be worthwhile teachers. They are lessons of love, time, forgiveness, endurance, and a constant reformation.[10]

The "Rock of my heart" is that part of me that has learned (very slowly!) patience and resilience. It is my capacity for a kind of compassionate awareness, for being present with the truth of my life even in the moments when that truth is not so easy. If I can embrace the ups and downs of my experience, the pleasant and the difficult, the painful as well as the joyful, as "worthwhile teachers," then I can learn important lessons, and celebrate my own strength and endurance.

After describing YHVH as "Rock of my heart," Psalm 73 continues: *"For me, it is good to draw near to God; I have made YHVH my refuge."* To discover the "Rock of my heart," I need to be proactive, to "draw near" to the godly place of refuge within. Sometimes the "Rock of my heart" is covered by waves of anxiety or doubt, hidden from me. Spiritual practice is the means by which I can make it through and "draw near." To find refuge is not to hide away from the difficult truths of my life and of this moment. It is to develop the capacity to access the "Rock of my heart" when I most need it. Just as some rocks form in sedimentary layers over eons of time, so too my own capacity for compassionate awareness and wholesome action is the accumulation of many years of practice. Rock reminds us, in our "get it as fast as you can" world, that real wisdom cannot be gained instantaneously. We need to hang in there with ourselves, and with those around us, for true refuge to be found.

Rock of Ages

About one year after my spouse, Gina, died, a small group of family and friends gathered at the graveside for a Jewish ritual called "unveiling." We were dedicating the grave marker—a beautiful rose-colored granite headstone. It is traditional, once the marker has been erected, for visitors to leave pebbles on the grave. For the unveiling, I brought some of the small stones that Gina and I had collected on our various trips. It was very moving to watch those who loved Gina place one of these small markers of our life together on the gravestone. Even as her body was slowly returning to the earth, these little pieces of earth were now marking a connection between the living and the dead. In the years since, I still see these stones when I go to visit the grave, an ongoing reminder of the years we had together.

Since very ancient times, humans have used stones to mark important moments and places. There are tens of thousands of Neolithic standing stones found across the British Isles and Europe, some over twenty feet tall, their meaning mysterious. Standing stones have also been found in excavations of Bronze Age Palestine, marking sacred sites, burial spots, the site of covenant ceremonies, and more.

In the Hebrew Bible, stones are used to mark events and locations that have both spiritual and historical signif-icance. After Jacob's first encounter with YHVH, when he has his awe-inspiring dream, he takes the rock that served as his pillow and sets it up as a standing stone. He then anoints it with olive oil and names the spot Beit-El, the "House of God."[11] When Moses creates a covenant ritual after receiving the Torah at Mount Sinai, binding the Is-raelites to YHVH and to one another, he builds an altar and sets up twelve standing stones, representing the twelve tribes of Israel.[12] In the book of Joshua, when the Israelites finally cross over the Jordan River into the promised land, a leader of each tribe takes a stone from the river and sets it up as a sign of their crossing. Joshua tells the people that these stones will be a marker for future generations to remember this long-awaited moment.[13]

In January 2020, I visited sites in Georgia and Alabama connected to the history of the struggle for African American freedom and equality. In Selma, Alabama, I learned about the 1960s campaign for voting rights in a state where, due to violent repression and intimidation, only 2 percent of Black citizens were registered to vote. In the winter of 1965, when a local activist, Jimmie Lee Jackson, was murdered by a state trooper during a nonviolent voting rights march in nearby Marion, civil rights leaders called for a march from Selma to the state capital of Montgomery. As local activists attempted to begin their march by crossing over the Edmund Pettus Bridge, they were viciously attacked by white troopers and posse members. This event, Bloody Sunday, was followed by more anti-Black violence in the days after, and galvanized national support for the march. With the backing of President Johnson and the protection of federal troops, hundreds of civil rights activists, led by Dr. Martin Luther King Jr., made their way to the capitol in Montgomery.

Today, on the far side of the Edmund Pettus Bridge, there is a memorial park dedicated to the incredibly brave individuals involved in the march and the larger struggle for voting rights. It includes a large gray boulder, etched with these words from the biblical book of Joshua: *"When your children shall ask you in the time to come, saying, 'What mean these 12 stones?' then you shall tell them how you made it over."*[14] This modern standing stone makes a powerful connection between the Israelites' arrival in the promised land and the significance of the Selma-to-Montgomery march in the struggle for American democracy.

In Montgomery, I visited the Legacy Museum of the Equal Justice Initiative (EJI), which explores the historical context that gave rise to the civil rights movement, from slavery through segregation, and the ongoing injustice of mass incarceration in America. The museum documents the violence used to enforce white supremacy after the Civil War, and the accompanying National Memorial for Peace and Justice is dedicated to the memory of the thousands of Black people lynched in the U.S. from 1877 through 1950. The EJI is both lifting up the history of these public acts of racial terror, intended to intimidate the African American

community in the Deep South and beyond, while also mo-
bilizing communities where lynching occurred to acknowledge this history as part of the healing process. In the
museum and at the lynching memorial, you can see walls
of jars containing earth from counties across the country,
each one labeled with the name of the person murdered on
that spot, collected by local citizens.

On another continent, the German artists Gunter Dem-
nig and Michael Friedrichs-Friedländer have crafted and
installed over seventy thousand "stumbling stones"—
Stolpersteine—in cities across Europe and Russia, marking
the last known places of residence of Jews, Roma, disabled
people, and other victims of the Nazi regime. These small
brass "stones" are engraved with the name, date of birth,
and fate of the person being remembered—whether suicide,
exile, or most commonly deportation and murder. The project, which began in 1996, calls on local groups to research
those who were victimized, raise money to install the
"stumbling stone," and find as many of the memorialized
person's living relatives as possible to invite to the instal-
lation ceremony. The project honors the memory of those
targeted by the Nazis in such a way that one might "stumble" across the painful history while simply walking down
the street. Like the jars filled with earth in the Legacy Museum, the Stolpersteine memorialize both the preciousness

of individual human lives and the unspeakable violence of which humanity is capable.

The lessons of memory and of witness, captured in stone and earth, are important for any society trying to acknowledge the injustices and injuries of its past and its present. These memorials can lift up, as well, the legacy of resistance to that injustice. In her exquisite poem "Invocation," carved into a stone pillar at the National Memorial for Peace and Justice, Elizabeth Alexander writes:

Your names were never lost,
each name a holy word.
The rocks cry out—
call out each name to sanctify this place . . .

Ancestors, you will find us still in cages,
despised and disciplined.
You will find us still mis-named.

Here you will find us despite.
You will not find us extinct.
You will find us here memoried and storied.[15]

If stones and earth can be used to create powerful memorials and historical markers, so can the metaphor of God as Rock help us understand how connected each of us is to those with whom we share our world. The "Rock of Ages" is that which holds our history, whether on a geological or a human time scale. This name of God—*Tzur Olamim*—can also be translated as "Rock of Many Worlds." In the earthiness that each of us shares with every being, animate and inanimate, on this rock orbiting around the sun, we are invited to connect our own personal "world" to the many other "worlds" around us. We can learn that our fates are interconnected: whether as citizens of a nation with a complex and fraught history; as individuals vulnerable to the violence of dictatorship and war; or as interdependent denizens of this planet. In the words of Arthur Walker-Jones:

> God as Rock is a resource from the Hebrew Bible that represents a radical shift in perspective. It may help us to imagine a more livable reality in which humanity is part of a sacred, interdependent and living Earth community made up of many diverse human and nonhuman subjects.[16]

Mother Rock

There is one place in the Torah, the first five books of the Bible, that God is called *Rock*. It comes near the very end of Deuteronomy, in a long poem that Moses recites to the Israelites on the border of the promised land. Moses knows that he will not be going in with them, and these verses are among his final words to the community he has spent the past forty years guiding through the desert.

In the opening of the poem, Moses declares, *"I will call out the name of YHVH, praise the greatness of our God—the Rock, Its actions are wholesome, all Its ways are justice."*[17] Moses goes on to relate how the people have been cared for by YHVH, yet they have rebelled, forgetting all that God—the Rock of their salvation[18]—has done for them. And it is here, in the description of God's care and the people's ignorance, that we get a whole new way of thinking about God as Rock:

> *YHVH alone did lead [you] . . . made [you] ride on the heights of the land, fed [you] the produce of the fields. [YHVH] suckled you with honey from the craggy stone, and oil from the rock . . . But you neglected the Rock that bore you, and forgot God who birthed you.*[19]

Beginning with the image of the Israelites being "suckled," like a baby, with honey and olive oil flowing from rocks, to the striking metaphor of God as a Rock that gave birth to them, we are introduced to the idea of God as a

Mother Rock. It is unclear what the image of honey and oil flowing from rocks might have literally referred to. One possibility may have been the honeycomb of hives of wild bees found in the crags of mountain rocks, and the olive oil that flowed from stone oil presses. Or perhaps the reference was to the ability of the rocky land of Canaan to nurture date and olive trees (the "honey" mentioned in the Torah often refers to date syrup). Either way, this image of the people being nursed like a baby with such rich and delicious foods from the loving breast of the Mother Rock is quite marvelous.

Rock as the source of communal sustenance finds an echo in an earlier episode in the Exodus story, right after the Israelites have escaped from slavery in Egypt. Out in the desert, the people lack water and food. They complain loudly to Moses, accusing him of bringing them out of Egypt just to kill them with thirst. Moses cries out to God for help and receives these somewhat strange instructions:

> *YHVH said to Moses: Go before the people and take some of the elders of Israel with you; and take the rod with which you struck the Nile river, and go. Here I am standing before you, there on the rock at Horev. Strike the rock, and water will come out of it, and the people will drink.*[20]

Moses does as instructed, and the crisis is (momentarily) resolved. But what can we make of this image of God standing on the rock that Moses is supposed to hit with his staff? Is God somehow in the rock? A divine Presence surrounding it? It's all a bit mysterious, but what is important for our purposes is this association of God with a rock that produces water for the thirsty Israelites. Like the rocks of Moses's song which produce honey and oil, this rock is a source of sustenance in the wilderness. All are associated with YHVH's bounty and care for the people.

Rock as refuge, as strength, as nurturing breast—all of these associations combine to suggest Something to which we can turn for support, protection, and nourishment. This Rock holds us, connects us, grounds us in the truth of our own lives, and in the godly soil of wholeness and justice.

God as Rock Practice

As recorded in the Psalms, singing and speaking to the Rock appears to have been something our biblical ancestors did as part of their spiritual practice, whether asking "my Rock and my Redeemer" to accept their meditations and words of prayer (Psalm 19:15), crying out to "my Rock" and asking that It not be unresponsive to their pleas (Psalm 28:1), speaking directly to "my Rock" and asking to be remembered and helped (Psalm 42:10), or "making a joyful noise" to "the Rock of our salvation" (Psalm 95:1). These verses suggest two practices to bring alive this metaphor:

Sing to the Rock;

The artist and activist Melanie DeMore has a simple, powerful song called "Standing Stone," which you can hear and sing along with on her CD *In The Mother House,* or find on YouTube. Written for a friend of hers who was dealing with stage 4 cancer, Ms. DeMore says that "I wrote this song because sometimes all we can do is stand by each other. That is all we can do." The words are:

I will be your standing stone
I will stand by you

She suggests holding someone in mind who is suffering as you sing. You might also imagine the Rock of Refuge singing it to you.

Speak to the Rock: With the practice of *hitbodedut* described in chapter 5, try addressing God using one or more of the "rock names" found in the Hebrew Bible and Jewish liturgy. You might want to use these names if you find yourself in a particularly hard time or situation, if you are feeling anxious or adrift. Here are some of the names:

- *Tzur Yisheynu*—Rock of Salvation (or Rock of Liberation)
- *Tzur Y'lad'cha*—Birth Rock (or Mama Rock)
- *Tzur Chayyenu*—Rock of Life
- *Tzuri* or *Sal'i*—My Rock
- *Tzur Olamim*—Rock of Ages (or Everlasting Rock)
- *Tzur Ma'on*—Rock of Refuge
- *Tzur Uzi*—Rock of my strength
- *Tzur Levavi*—Rock of my heart
- *Tzuri v'Go'ali*—My Rock and my Redeemer

As you do the *hitbodedut* practice, speaking from your heart to the Rock, you might want to hold in your hand or have laid out in front of you some stones that you've collected. Don't underestimate how comforting it can be to hold on to a firm stone as you seek a bit of balance and steadiness in your life.

Be for Me a Rock of Refuge

The idea of "refuge" is a powerful one, and it begs the question: What is real refuge, and how is it different from just hiding? I think of "hiding" as akin to the sheets-over-chairs "forts" that my brother and I would build in our house when we were little. We would bring all kinds of stuff into our fort with us, trying to make our alternative living space as viable as possible. But despite our protestations to our parents, at some point these forts had to come down, and we'd have to start all over again. Like kids in a makeshift fort, sometimes we all feel the need to find a cozy space that feels hidden away—from the terrors of the world, from difficulties in our lives, from stresses at home or work. Relief can come in the form of watching TV or going shopping, eating junk food or lighting up a joint. Done in moderation, this kind of hiding is not, in and of itself, particularly problematic. What *is* problematic is when any of our hiding behaviors become habitual or take over our lives. And like childhood forts, these hiding places are very temporary, and can't provide any lasting or meaningful refuge.

A true "Rock of refuge," on the other hand, is something deep, strong, and trustworthy. Ideally, it doesn't cost any money, and is accessible whenever we need it. This quality is captured in the book of Isaiah, when the prophet says, *"Be secure in YHVH always, for Yah YHVH is the Eternal Rock."*[21] Achieving this sense of steadiness and trust is one of the central goals of spiritual practice. Rabbi Sheila Peltz Weinberg describes true refuge as that which takes us out of the narrow place—of constricted heart and mind, of fear and aversion—into an expansive space, where we can act with clarity, wisdom, and compassion.

The following are a few simple exercises that can be doorways into a sense of refuge:

Mountain Pose and Rock of Ages Body Scan: The foundational pose in yoga is called *mountain pose,* and it is a simple standing pose that helps us feel grounded—connected to the earth and to our bodies. As an exploration of the metaphor of God as Rock, I am suggesting a practice combining this yoga pose with a wonderful guided meditation created by Dr. Jill Schneiderman, professor of geology. The meditation is intended to awaken in us a sense of the vastness of geologic time, and our own species' newness on the scene.[22] We can experience an embodied sense of *Tzur Olamim,* the Eternal Rock, in this meditation, as well as a sense of connection to the history of the earth of which we are a part. Dr. Schneiderman uses points along the body to give a sense of the distance between geological epochs. I recommend making a recording of these instructions and then playing the recording as you do the standing meditation (be sure to go slow and leave some pauses in between each part of the meditation). If you are new to yoga, you can find detailed instructions for mountain pose online—I've included some very basic instructions here:

Begin by taking off your shoes and socks, and placing your feet either together, or a few inches apart (no wider than hip width). Make sure your toes are pointing forward, and feel the balls and heels on the floor. Spread out your toes. Gently align your body, bringing your knees in line above your ankles, your hips in line with your knees (tuck your tailbone slightly), your shoulders in line with your hips, and your ears in line with your shoulders. Your arms are straight down by your sides, palms facing forward. Relax your shoulders away from your ears, and let your chest open. Breathe into your belly, and see if you can imagine your feet rooted in the ground. Feel yourself supported by the earth, your body attentive but relaxed. Imagine you are a mountain, firm and strong. Feel the power of *Tzur Uzi,* Rock of My Strength, within yourself. You can close your eyes, or gaze forward, focusing on a point in front of you. Stand for a minute or two, breathing in and out from your belly.

Now, set an intention to cultivate a feeling in the body—rather than an understanding in the mind—for the vastness of geologic time.

Feel the bottoms of your feet and take them to symbolize the earliest moments in the formation of Earth, over four billion years ago.

Next, bring your attention to the ankles and then halfway up your calves. At this midway point, picture the dynamic early solar system, when meteorites bombarded the planets.

Move from the calves up the legs, pausing at the knee joint, which stands for the oldest rocks that survive today. The knees' synovial fluid signifies the water vapor that condensed at this time to form Earth's early global ocean.

Bring the attention upward to the thighs, which represent the evolution of the earliest life on Earth—simple, single-celled organisms.

In this distance-for-time metaphor, approximately halfway up the length of the body, the pelvic bones mark the establishment of an oxygen-rich atmosphere.

Continuing to proceed upward along the length of the body, the navel marks where the first single-celled life containing distinct organelles evolved.

At the height of the chest is the spot that corresponds to the flourishing of, finally, soft-bodied multicellular life.

At the neck, one can envision the first appearance of animals with hard parts—trilobites and invertebrates that populated the seas. However, along the length of *only one head,* from the mouth to the eyes to the forehead and the scalp, we traverse the more familiar stages in Earth history—the ages of fishes and then reptiles and finally mammals.

A skullcap of ice represents the last glacial age.

Receiving Love Meditation: A powerful sense of refuge can be found in allowing ourselves to feel loved and cared for; it is a way to experience God as the loving "Rock of my heart." This meditation is based on the benefactor practice taught by Buddhist teacher and author John Makransky:

Begin by bringing to mind people whom you associate with love and care; they can be living or dead, or even people you admire but have never met. You might remember a moment with another person in which you experienced connection, comfort, or care. You can also call to mind a beloved pet. If it is difficult to summon up people, think of a place in which you feel particularly safe and at ease, or where you feel inspired and alive. These people, pets, moments, and/or places are your "benefactors."

To enter into the meditation: Sit in a relaxed yet alert

way, on a cushion or in a chair. Having identified your benefactor(s) or benefactor moment, bring this to mind and imagine their smiling faces (or a special place) before you. Envision the benefactor sending you the wish of love, the wish for your deepest well-being, happiness, and joy. Imagine their wish as a gentle energy, a soft radiance, like a tender shower of healing rays. Bathe your whole body and mind in that tender radiance, all the way down to your toes and fingertips. Let your cells soak in the wishes of well-being. Take it into your heart.

Bask in the gentle, healing energy of that radiance. As other thoughts or feelings arise, let them be enveloped in that loving luminosity. If you experience resistance, see if you can just accept the benefactors' wish for your deepest happiness. Be at ease, open and accepting, like a puppy lying in the morning sun, passively soaking up its rays. Bathe in this, heal in this, rest in this.

After a little while, join your benefactors in their wish for you. While receiving the energy of their love, mentally repeat the wish for yourself: "May this one have deepest well-being, happiness, and joy." Affirm the words repeatedly in your mind. "May this one have deepest well-being, happiness, and joy." Try to mean the words as you say them, like your benefactors mean them for you. Repeat the wish for yourself while receiving your benefactors' love even more deeply into your body and mind.

For the final few minutes of the meditation, you can let go of the images and the words, and just sit, feeling a sense of comfort and ease. You may want to rest a hand on your heart, sending it a blessing of steadiness, of love, emanating from *Tzur Levavi,* the Rock of my heart.

7

• • • • •

THE GOD-CLOUD

In the early months of 2020, I was on sabbatical, taking a few months off from my congregational work to focus on writing this book. I returned on March 10, just in time for the Jewish holiday of Purim and a big Purim party. Five days later, the congregation—along with much of Massachusetts—was physically shut down, due to the COVID-19 pandemic.

Those first few weeks brought many challenges and a lot of learning. I had to figure out how to lead Shabbat services via Zoom; how to guide and comfort congregants unable to be physically present with their ill and dying parents; how to create bnei mitzvah ceremonies with me in one place and the family in another. The question that accompanied me in all of my work with my congregation was this: How do we foster a sense of closeness—to one another, to our community, to Jewish practice—when we can't be physically close?

That spring, as I taught a Zoom class about God in Metaphor, I realized that this same question was very much alive for my biblical ancestors. They seem to have experienced YHVH as a Presence that could be closely felt, yet could not be held in a material object, in an idol made of metal or wood or clay. The divine could be glimpsed but not fully seen, heard but not entirely comprehended, encountered but not contained. With the metaphor of Cloud, the biblical authors found a way to convey a sense of nearness to Something close by that cannot be touched.

Cloud by Day and Fire by Night

As they left the bondage of Egypt, the Torah recounts that the fleeing Israelites were accompanied by YHVH as *"a column of cloud by day, to guide them along the way, and in a column of fire by night, to give them light, that they might travel day and night."*[1] When Pharaoh's army came chasing after them, *"the messenger of God that was going before the camp of Israel moved and went behind them; and the column of cloud moved from in front of them and stood behind them, coming between the camp of Egypt and the camp of Israel.*"[2]

The language here is interesting. When the column of cloud is first mentioned, we're told that YHVH "went" or "walked" within it. In the next mention, it appears that the column of cloud is itself God's "messenger." A few verses later, we're told that YHVH looked out at the Egyptian army from within the column, throwing them into a panic as they drove their chariots into the Red Sea.[3] Taken all together, these texts suggest that God's presence was made known to the Israelites (and to the Egyptians) through this imposing column of cloud and fire.

The column of cloud and fire becomes an ongoing feature of the Israelites' journey through the wilderness (we will explore the metaphor of Fire in more depth in the next chapter). In Psalm 105, a retelling the Exodus narrative, we are told that YHVH "*spread a cloud for a covering, and a fire to give light in the night.*"[4] The prophet Nehemia describes the column of cloud as a sign of YHVH's love for the people: "*You, in Your abundant lovingkindness, did not abandon them in the wilderness. The column of cloud did not depart from them by day to lead them on the way, nor the column of fire by night to give them light on their path.*"[5] And at the end of the book of Exodus, as Moses completes the construction of the Mishkan, the sanctuary in the wilderness, an *anan YHVH*—literally a "God cloud"—appears over it, signifying YHVH's presence amid the Israelite camp.[6]

The "cloud by day" seems to have offered a few important things to the Israelites as they made their way through the wilderness. At the Sea of Reeds, it was a protective barrier, coming between the Israelites and the pursuing Egyptian army. As a "covering" during their journey, it offered shelter from the scorching desert sun. And perhaps most importantly in a desert region, a cloud indicated the availability of water.[7] Along with the warmth and light of the column of fire at night, the column of cloud by day was a sign of divine nurturance, protection, and presence.

Making Visible What Is Invisible

During a family vacation in Puerto Rico, Gina and I took our kids for a hike in El Yunque National Forest, a tropical rainforest in the Luquillo Mountains. It is a beautiful area, sacred to the indigenous Taino people. We climbed up the El Yunque peak, and, arriving at the top, felt disappointed when we couldn't see anything at all. The view was completely obscured by clouds as we sat and rested on the rocks. We were about to give up and head back when, all

of a sudden, the clouds swept away, and we found ourselves gazing at a magnificent panorama. A few minutes
later, the clouds returned, and we could barely see a foot
in front of us. Dense fog, and then a view, fog, and then
view—this magical oscillation continued as we sat within
the cloud.

It is in the nature of clouds to obscure things from view
while also making something that is usually invisible visible. As the folks at NASA explain:

> Water vapor is always in the sky in some amount but is in-
> visible. Clouds form when an area of air becomes cooler
> until the water vapor there condenses to liquid form. At
> that point, the air is said to be "saturated" with water va-
> por. The air where the cloud forms must be cool enough
> for the water vapor to condense. The water will condense
> around things like dust, ice or sea salt—all known as con-
> densation nuclei. The temperature, wind and other
> conditions where a cloud forms determine what type of
> cloud it will be.[8]

The authors of the Bible most likely did not know all
of the science behind the formation of clouds, but they
understood an aspect of reality that this scientific definition of clouds makes clear: that something life-sustaining

and ever-present (whether water vapor or the divine) can be both unseen and very much there. Indeed, it is when the water vapor in the atmosphere both cools down and interacts with other objects in the atmosphere—dust, ice, salt—that it becomes visible as a cloud. So too the biblical texts about God as Cloud imply that YHVH's invisible presence becomes visible when It interacts with human beings.

In the book of Numbers, there is an interesting interchange between Moses and YHVH, as Moses reminds God of God's special relationship with the Israelites:

> *[The other nations] have heard that You, YHVH, are in the midst of this people, for You, YHVH, are seen eye to eye while Your cloud stands over them.*[9]

It is somewhat startling that Moses makes the claim that God is seen "eye to eye" by the Israelites. Moses's words suggest an extremely close encounter of humans with the divine. This closeness is signified by the presence of God's "cloud standing over them." Moses's words about God's relationship with the people echoes his own experience of intimate encounter, similarly involving the divine cloud:

> *When Moses entered the Tent of Meeting, the column of cloud would descend and stand at the entrance of the*

*Tent and speak with Moses . . . And YHVH would speak
to Moses face to face, as a person speaks to their friend.*[10]

"Eye to eye" and "face to face"—in these texts, the metaphor of God's face meeting the face of beloved human
beings is connected to the visible presence of a cloud. Over
and over again in the Torah, when YHVH appears to human beings (literally, "becomes seen"), it is in the form of a
cloud. One dramatic example is the moment of revelation
at Mount Sinai, when Moses ascends the mountain to receive the tablets of the covenant:

*Moses went up the mountain, and the cloud covered the
mountain. The Presence of YHVH rested on Mount Sinai,
and the cloud covered it for six days, and [God] called to
Moses on the seventh day from the midst of the cloud . . .
Moses went inside the cloud and ascended the mountain;
and Moses remained on the mountain forty days and forty
nights.*[11]

Later in the book of Exodus, when Moses goes back up
Mount Sinai to ask for forgiveness after the Israelites make
the golden calf, he begs to see God. YHVH answers that it
is not possible for a human to see the divine directly and
live, but promises a different kind of revelation: *"So Moses*

carved two tablets of stone like the first, and early in the morning he went up on Mount Sinai, as YHVH had commanded him . . . YHVH came down in a cloud and stood with him there, and proclaimed the name YHVH."[12]

There are also moments of conflict and tension during the Israelites' journey through the wilderness, when the God-Cloud suddenly appears to the entire community. No sooner have they made it through the Sea of Reeds when the Israelites start complaining that they're hungry and thirsty, and that life was better back in Egypt! Moses tells his brother, Aaron, to tell the people to "come close" to YHVH, for God has heard their grumbling. Then, "*as Aaron spoke to the whole Israelite community, they turned toward the wilderness, and here, YHVH's Presence appeared to them in a cloud.*"[13] In another episode, when Miriam and Aaron complain about Moses's special status, YHVH suddenly speaks to all three of the siblings, telling them to come out to the Tent of Meeting. And then: "*YHVH came down in a column of cloud, and stood by the door of the Tent, and called 'Aaron and Miriam!' and they both went out.*"[14]

I bring all of these examples to make the point that YHVH appearing in or as a cloud was a key way that the biblical authors expressed a tangible sense of God's presence. Just as water vapor is always present in the air, yet only becomes visible as a cloud when certain conditions are met, so too, the Torah suggests, with human experience of the divine. Whether at a very public moment, as at Mount Sinai, or in an intimate encounter, as with Moses, the God-Cloud reveals that when it comes to human affairs, God may be a bit closer than we realize.

Going into the Cloud

Rows and floes of angel hair
And ice cream castles in the air
And feather canyons everywhere
I've looked at clouds that way
But now they only block the sun
They rain and snow on everyone

—*Joni Mitchell, "Both Sides Now"*

While the divine cloud expresses a sense of God's presence, there are times when the appearance of the cloud is more foreboding than reassuring. One of those times was at Mount Sinai, as the Israelites awaited the great revelation. The experience of thunder and lightning and loud sounds frightened the people, and they *"stood at a distance,"* but *"Moses approached the thick cloud where God was."*[15]

The thick God-cloud on Sinai is not like the reassuring

column of cloud that accompanied the Israelites on their journey. It's not the airy angel hair of the Joni Mitchell song but the sign of a violent storm about to break. Yet Moses is undeterred: he walks right into the dark, dense cloud.

The eighteenth-century Hasidic master Rebbe Nachman of Bratslav understood this scene as a teaching about the obstacles we encounter on the spiritual path:

> The obstacle is like a thick cloud . . . This is the meaning of the verse *"So the people stood at a distance."* When they see the thick cloud, namely the obstacle, they remain at a distance. But Moses, who represents the quality of awareness for all of Israel, *"approached the thick cloud, where God was,"* namely: he approached the obstacle, where the blessed God is actually hidden.[16]

For Rebbe Nachman, the Israelites represent a normal state of consciousness—that is, most of us on most days. In the presence of something that appears to us to be an obstacle, the natural tendency is to back away. Moses, however, represents the "quality of awareness," a different kind of understanding. Moses realizes that what appears to others as daunting or difficult contains God's presence, and so he goes toward it.

In Buddhist teachings, the obstacles or "hindrances"

are those naturally occurring states of mind that get in the way of our being fully present in the moment. They include agitation or anxiety; lethargy; greed or grasping; aversion; and doubt. When we try to meditate and either can't sit still or we fall asleep; when all we can think about is an annoying sound or an enticing smell; when we decide we're just no good at meditation—all of these common reactions are the hindrances at play. And what happens in our meditation practice is what we experience in life. We get bored or antsy when nothing exciting is happening; we push unpleasant feelings away and crave anything that gives us momentary pleasure; we doubt our ability to ever grow or change—these are all obstacles on our path toward wholeness and peace. The hindrances operate by distracting us from our actual experience. Like the "thick cloud" on Sinai, they obscure our ability to see what is actually happening in our minds and hearts.

A number of years ago, I was on my annual weeklong silent retreat. After a few days of being unwell, I finally felt better, and I was eagerly looking forward to lunch. I got my food and went to sit at a table outdoors in the sunshine. I was prepared to have a magnificent experience, eating slowly and mindfully, experiencing marvelous tastes and sensations, as I had on many retreats past.

A minute later, another retreat participant sat down

opposite me at the picnic table. He proceeded to pick up an apple and take a bite. It was the loudest sound I had ever heard. He took another bite. I felt like I was in a special-effects studio—there was no way a normal human mouth could make that much noise biting into an apple. I tried to return my awareness to my own eating, but then he took another earsplitting bite.

I abandoned hope of my perfect retreat meal. I began calculating how many bites a person could take of the outside of an apple, because I figured it was those outside, through-the-skin bites that had the most sound value. He had already taken three. I calculated there couldn't be more than another three or so. I would wait patiently for him to finish, and then resume my meal. I don't know how it was physically possible, but the crunching went on for at least another ten minutes. He ate every last bite of that apple, and every bite had the sonic quality of a car crash to my ears.

I thought about getting up and finding a different spot, but that just ignited a new chain reaction of dismay. Wouldn't it be obvious to this man that I was disgusted with the noise he was making? I didn't want to hurt his feelings. And what about my mindfulness practice—shouldn't I be able to overcome this mild annoyance and achieve a state of calm acceptance? I was a total failure as a meditator if I got up and left. Besides, I loved this spot. I was there first. He was the one who wasn't being mindful, wasn't paying attention to the effect of his actions on others, wasn't really eating that apple in a very meditative way. I wasn't going to move.

While even in the moment I was able to see a bit of humor in the situation, I really was very disappointed and sad that my meal had been ruined. But this is where the learning happened. My meal hadn't actually been ruined— just my fantasy of what I wanted my meal to be. I had absolutely no idea, if the apple man hadn't been there, what I would have experienced. Maybe I would have gotten distracted. Maybe the taste of the food wouldn't have been so marvelous. Maybe I would have spilled my plate all over myself. Or maybe it would have been the most profound experience of eating I'd ever had in my life. But all of those were just imagined possibilities. The only meal I actually had was this one: sitting at a table in the sunshine, across from a man eating an apple. The actual experience was mildly unpleasant. It was my frantic desire for it to be other than what it is was that made me miserable. I couldn't really taste my food or enjoy the summer air because I was so preoccupied figuring out how and when this unpleasantness would end.

This is just one simple example of the hindrances at

play. My aversion to the reality of my own experience, my intense desire to have what was actually happening not be happening, made me unhappy. The more I tried to push that reality away, to make it other than it was, the unhappier I got. This is where Rebbe Nachman's teaching comes in:

> One who is aware can find God in the midst of the obstacles themselves. There really are not any obstacles in the world at all, because in the obstacles themselves is found the Holy One. Through the obstacles themselves, in fact, one might draw closer to God because that is where God is hidden. And this is the meaning of "*Moses approached the thick cloud*": that is the obstacle, for that is "*where God was.*"

Commenting on this teaching, Rabbi Sheila Peltz Weinberg writes:

> When we get into an adversarial relationship with our own experience, we notice that the unpleasantness of the experience is exacerbated. It is like picking a scab. Awareness is restricted . . . The practice of mindfulness is the alternative strategy pointed to in our text. We can choose to enter the frightening or difficult experience. We can choose to draw near, to not run away, and to resist the

mental habits. Moses represents the quality of mindful-ness, which is non-judgmental awareness moment to mo-ment. There is no pushing away and no holding back.[17]

Rebbe Nachman's invitation to us is to realize that Godliness is present in "both sides" of clouds, the pleas-ant and the difficult. What first appears as an obstacle can become an opportunity for awareness and connection. As Rabbi Weinberg teaches, mindfulness practice is a power-ful tool to foster the capacity to sit with what is, to come close to our experience with a calm, loving awareness. But even if we do not have a formal meditation practice, it is possible to take the invitation to "go into the thick cloud."

When a challenging moment arises, we can pause, and notice our reaction. Do I want to pull away? Lash out? By breathing for a moment, and noticing what is happening inside myself, I can short-circuit the feedback loop of aver-sion. One way to do this is to shift my attention from the situation and my thoughts about it to the sensations in my body. Where am I feeling the sadness, or anger, or fear? This is a way to make room for the experience, instead of pushing it away. Notice if there is tightness or any other sensation in the throat, or belly, or chest. See what hap-pens when you notice it; keep breathing. Then, like Moses walking into the cloud, turn *toward* what you are feeling, not away. You can even say to yourself, "This is where God is." By going "into the cloud," we can often discover a truth that awaits us, and from that place, we can act with clarity and wisdom.

Look at the Sky

During those first weeks of the pandemic shutdown, the world around me got very quiet. As businesses closed and traffic stopped, it was possible to go outside and really hear the birds. While my work ramped up, I still had a sense that the world around me was slowing down. During my class, as we explored texts about God as Cloud, I asked my congregants to reflect on their own experiences with clouds. This is what one person shared:

A few years ago, I heard a New Year's resolution from someone who said her hope was to "look up" every day. She felt she spent too much time narrowly focused on the mundane aspects of life—home, work, family, related worries, issues, plans, etc. She decided that she would spend time looking up at the sky, noticing clouds. She put a beautiful photo of clouds on her phone screen so she would see it anytime she picked up her phone. I tried this and noticed that it changed my mindset pretty quickly. I can't describe it exactly but for some reason, just looking up at the sky helped me change my perspective. Maybe it seemed like my problems suddenly seemed less dramatic, smaller.

Over two hundred years before my congregant learned the power of "looking up at the sky," this story was told about our friend Rebbe Nachman of Bratslav:

From his window facing the marketplace, Rebbe Nachman spotted one of his followers rushing by. "Have you looked up at the sky this morning?" the Rebbe asked.

"No, Rebbe, I haven't had the time."

"Believe me, in fifty years everything you see here today will be gone. There will be another fair—with other horses, other wagons, different people. I won't be here then and neither will you. So what's so important that you don't have time to look at the sky?!"[18]

The context of the Rebbe Nachman story is that this particular disciple used to come to town to sit and learn

Torah with his beloved rabbi. As he became more successful in business, he no longer came to learn, instead heading
straight to the market to attend to buying and selling. This
was what Rebbe Nachman was responding to when he saw
him rushing by. What is interesting is that Rebbe Nachman
didn't say, "Hey! What happened to learning Torah?" Instead, he reminded his student to look at the sky. Perhaps
he was saying: "Stop. Notice this beautiful world of which
you are a part. Take a moment to get some perspective.
Are you doing what you really want to be doing with your
life? Are you happy? Are you running toward something
worthwhile, or perhaps you're running away from something else?"

You could say that Rebbe Nachman was reminding
his student to pay attention to that which is eternal—the
heavens—versus all that is ephemeral here on earth, including ourselves. In contrast, my congregant's reflection
continued:

> Clouds change quickly. One moment the sky can be cloud-
> less. Look up again, and clouds are moving in. It shows
> us that things can change quickly. They may be dark at
> one moment, but the sun returns . . . I've been outside
> at times when it's been really dark and cloudy. Suddenly
> some rays of light break through. The world seems trans-

formed and more safe/secure/happy—inspired, almost. I am reminded that life is always changing, not always cloudy or always sunny. Without the contrast of clouds and light, I wouldn't see this.

It is wonderful to know that we can radically shift our perspective simply by looking up at the sky. Looking at clouds, we are able to experience the most basic truth of our existence: that things change, moment to moment. The sun may be covered over for a long time; we may go through truly heartbreaking experiences in our lives. But even in the midst of heartbreak, the clouds move and shift. A moment of gratitude can punctuate grief, just as a ray of sunlight can shine through the clouds. The discovery of inner resilience and strength can emerge from the depths of pain. If, as my congregant suggests in her reflection, we can embrace the reality of ongoing, never-ending change, we will suffer less, and sometimes experience exquisite joy. Perhaps *that* was the reality that Rebbe Nachman was pointing to when he told his student, "Look at the sky." Grasping at wealth, seeking security in the marketplace—these things bring no lasting satisfaction (which is why there is always the need to get more, more, more). Only by being like the clouds, flowing with the ever-changing winds, is it possible to achieve a modicum of peace. Look at the sky.

God as Cloud Practice

Look at the Sky: The instruction to "look at the sky" is a beautiful way to gain perspective on our lives, and a wonderful way to practice gratitude. A seventeenth-century rabbi, Yechiel Michel Epstein, recommended getting up and going to a window as soon as we're awake, to remind ourselves of the inherent holiness of all of Creation. He wrote:

> When you get up, look out your window at the sky and the earth and recall the verse *"Lift up your eyes on high and see—who created all this?"* (Isaiah 40:26). And think, *"How many are your works, YHVH, with wisdom have You made them all; the earth is full of Your creations"* (Psalm 104:24). Think of how wonderful Creation is, the sky and the earth and all that is in them—plants, animals, humans, creatures great and wonderful.[19]

Every morning I look out of one of my bedroom windows and I recite the two biblical verses that Rabbi Epstein recommends. I call this my "window practice." Try going to a window first thing in the morning, and look at the sky. Take a moment to notice the clouds and then whatever else is in view—trees, buildings, people. If you'd like, recite one or both of the verses that Rabbi Epstein recommends, or use other words that wake you up to the power and beauty of the sky and the earth.

If you're not a morning person, try to remember to go outside and look up at the sky at least once a day. Notice the clouds, or the absence of clouds. Let your mind, just for a moment or two, open as wide as the sky.

Like a Passing Cloud: As my congregant noted in her reflection, clouds are a wonderful reminder of the constantly changing nature of things. When we are inside a cloud, it eludes our grasp. When we watch clouds in the sky, we see them move and change shape from moment to moment. Clouds are an ongoing lesson in one very basic fact of our existence: everything comes and goes. All of creation is impermanent. We know this, of course, but we resist it mightily. And in that resistance, we suffer. We compound the natural sadness that we feel at the death of a beloved with an unwillingness to accept the truth of our mortality. We try to resist the very natural changes that occur—in our bodies, in our relationships, in our own hearts and minds—out of a deep desire that things remain the same. The truth is that change is hard, transitions are unsettling, and endings are often painful. And in resisting that truth, we make things worse.

The good news is that we can learn from clouds, and train ourselves to both understand and accept the basic impermanence of all things. Indeed, the Buddha taught that an awareness of this truth is an essential step on the path to ending suffering. To embrace the wisdom of clouds, we simply need to learn to notice what is happening around us all the time.

You can do this practice in many ways: while sitting in meditation, or taking a walk, or doing the dishes. The practice is simply this: pay attention to beginnings and endings. If you are sitting in meditation, notice a sound as it arises, and as it passes away. If you are walking, pay attention as objects—trees, cars, buildings—come into view, and as they fade from view. If you are washing dishes, notice the sensations in your hands, how one sensation arises, and changes, and another sensation begins. Practice this for a few days, picking a time during the day, or an activity, during which you will pay attention to sensations as they arise, and change, and pass away.

Once you have begun this practice, you can bring your attention to your own mind-states and emotions. Notice when joy arises, and how it changes. Do the same for sadness, or anger, or any other emotion. Try not to get caught up in the story that accompanies the emotion; simply pay attention to its arising and passing (even if it takes a while to move on).

Many years ago, at a session with a therapist, I told her that I couldn't really sit still, because when I sat still, I got anxious. The therapist replied, "Maybe you're anxious all the time, and you just notice it when you are sitting still?" I found this sort of funny, but most likely true. She invited me to sit with the anxiety, and see what happened. And what happened was that when I was able to just sit still, I felt the anxiety, which was unpleasant. But I continued to sit with it, and then it passed away. I wasn't done with anxiety—it's arisen again and again and again, countless times since that therapy session. But what I learned from that experience is that my anxiety—like any other mind-state—is not permanent. Like everything else, it arises and passes, if I can simply let it be. And with that realization, its power over me was lessened. I am not my anxiety, just like I am not my sadness, or my happiness, or my anger, or my confusion. These emotions and mind-states come and go, and I am able to stay steady in their passing.

Sometimes, of course, we suffer pain, either mental or physical, that is unrelenting, that does not come to an end on its own. In those situations, it is wise to seek medical or other kinds of interventions. But for so much of what we face in life, an ability to know that all things arise and pass is an incredible relief. We become less attached to the stories we tell ourselves about "how things are"—like my story about my anxiety—and become aware of what is actually happening. We can watch the clouds gather, feel the rain, and rejoice in the sun when it shines again.

Going into the Thick Cloud: I received this meditation instruction from Rabbi Sheila Peltz Weinberg, a wonderful teacher of mindfulness practice from a Jewish perspective. It helps develop the capacity to "go into" difficult emotions and mind-states, enabling us to turn toward, instead of away from, the obstacles to being present in the moment. In this version, I have incorporated imagery from our exploration of God as Cloud:

Find a seat in a comfortable, alert position. Close your eyes. Relax the eyes, face, neck. You can take one or two deep breaths, releasing tension on the out-breath. Become aware of the sensations of your body sitting, noticing where your body touches the chair, the floor. Be gentle with your mind, noticing thoughts as if they are wisps of cloud floating across the sky. Sit for a minute or two without trying to do anything in particular, just noticing your body, your breath, and letting go of thoughts as they arise as best you can.

Now, bring your attention to your breath. As you breathe

in, imagine that the space around your heart is becoming expansive, unbounded. Breathe in a sense of spaciousness in your chest, in your entire body. You can imagine yourself sitting in a cloud, or a cloud sitting within you—light, expansive, protective. Invite into yourself a sense of ease, of openness, of gentleness.

When you are ready, bring to mind something in your life that frightens you or that angers you. It does not have to be the greatest fear or the greatest annoyance. Something small will suffice. Notice images or words that might be forming in your mind as you bring this to mind.

Now bring your attention back to the breath. See what your breath is like. See if you can locate the fear or the anger somewhere in the sensations of your body. As you do this, see if you can keep a very expanded sense of awareness, an expanded sense of your body, a sense of the cloud both surrounding and supporting the difficult experience.

Notice the sensations of fear or anger where they appear in that vast openness. Do you feel any tightness or heat in the chest, the throat, the belly? Do you notice any sensations of aliveness? Of constriction? Let your awareness rest in these sensations—without having to describe or analyze, just be aware.

Try to drop the story of the fear, of the anger. Try not to add to the thoughts. Allow the thoughts to fade into the vast openness without pursuing them. Just notice sensations. They may be unpleasant. Notice if you can allow them to be present without judging them or pushing them away. See if they change without your making them change. Just be present in this moment to what is happening. Allow the breath to come and go and pass through any place of discomfort. Just stay with the breath. Breathing in and out. Notice what is arising and passing.

If you would like, invite God's presence into this space. You might imagine yourself sitting under or inside a beautiful, sheltering cloud. Rest your awareness in the sensations of your body, the sensations of your breath, the expansiveness within you and around you. When you are ready, open your eyes.

Making the Invisible Visible: In the Hebrew Bible, God as Cloud was a way to express a tangible sense of God's presence in the absence of the concrete reminders—idols—that were common in the surrounding cultures. We skeptical modern folks are in a somewhat similar situation to the authors of the Bible. If I can't see the divine, if I have no physical proof of Its existence, then how do I know It's there? How do I feel It, access It, know It?

One answer to those questions is a practice called spiritual direction. Developed in the Christian tradition, spiritual direction has been taken on by other religious communities.

Done either one-to-one or in small groups, spiritual direction is a facilitated conversation that helps the "directee" gain insight on where, and how, God is present in their life. Even as someone who thinks about God a lot, I have found spiritual direction enormously helpful in connecting whatever is happening in my life back to an exploration of the ways in which godliness is present. When I am feeling sad and lost, when I am seeking a sense of refuge, or when I need help navigating a challenging situation, the question "Where is God in this?" never fails to bring new insights.

It is possible to do spiritual direction in person or over the phone or internet. You don't necessarily need to find a director from your own religious tradition (I know a number of rabbis who have had wonderful experiences with nuns!). There are networks of spiritual directors in most Christian denominations, among Unitarian Universalists, and in the Muslim and Jewish worlds as well. On the website of Spiritual Directors International, you can find information about a broad range of what they call "spiritual companions." And you don't need to be a devout "believer" to gain benefit from spiritual direction. If you are seeking greater spiritual insight or an expanded sense of godliness in your life, it is worth giving spiritual direction a try. And I can attest that it's a great place to play with the metaphors in this book!

8

· · · · ·

HOLY FIRE

One winter weekend during rabbinical school, I took myself to a retreat center outside Philadelphia. I had never been on a silent retreat before, but I was yearning for some quiet time and space. I had a small one-room hut, nestled in a little grove of bamboo, all to myself. My main challenge was that I wasn't entirely sure what I should do on my self-initiated retreat. I found a book by the Buddhist teacher Thich Nhat Hanh and tried out his instructions for walking meditation. I prayed. I made some meals, heating up food I had brought, on a little hot plate. But what turned out to be my main activity on my mini-retreat was lighting a fire in the wood-burning stove, and then just sitting and staring at the flames.

There is something truly magical about watching a fire.

The pops and cracks of the wood as it burns, the dancing blue-and-orange flames; I know I am not the only person who finds it mesmerizing. As one biblical scholar notes, it is fire's quality of "overwhelming fascination" that contributes to its biblical association with the divine.[1] In fact, many cultures associate the realm of the sacred with fire. Perhaps fire-gazing in my little hut that wintry weekend was more of a spiritual practice than I even realized.

In the Torah, the Israelites kept their eyes on the divine column of fire that showed them the path on their nighttime travels. The fire lit their way through the wilderness, and also served as a sign of protection during the cold desert nights. The comforting nature of this fire is emphasized by Moses when he reminds the Israelites how they were carried lovingly through the wilderness by YHVH "*as a father carries a child,*" accompanied by the column of fire and cloud that went before them.[2]

Fire also figures prominently in YHVH's first appearance to Moses. As a young man, Moses fled Egypt and made his way to Midian. There he became a family man and a shepherd, leaving behind both his life in Pharaoh's palace and the travails of his Israelite kin. Fifty years after leaving Egypt, Moses is in for a surprise one day when he takes his flock out into the desert:

Moses was shepherding the sheep of Yitro his father-in-law . . . and he came to Horev, the mountain of God. And a messenger of YHVH appeared to him in a flame of fire in the midst of a bush. He looked, and behold, the bush was burning with fire, yet it was not consumed. And Moses said: "I will turn aside now, and see this great sight, why the bush is not burnt." And YHVH saw that he turned to look, and God called to him from within the bush, saying "Moses, Moses." And he said, "Here I am." And [God] said, "Do not come closer. Remove your sandals from your feet, for the place on which you stand is holy ground."[3]

While Moses's attention is caught by the odd, fascinating sight of a bush that is on fire yet not getting burned up, our attention as readers is directed to the fact that YHVH is somehow present in this fire. First we read that a *malakh*, a divine messenger, appears "in the flame of fire." A few verses later, YHVH calls to Moses from within the flaming bush. It is here, in his encounter with the divine Fire, that Moses learns that he is the one who will lead the Israelites out of slavery.

As the scene that sets in the motion the story of the Exodus, it is intriguing to me that God first appears to Moses "in the flame of fire." Presumably, there are many ways that

Moses might have had his first encounter with the divine. Why, of all things, a burning bush?

I once studied this text with a group of Jewish social justice activists, people who had dedicated their lives to bringing about a more caring, just society. I posed this question to them: In this pivotal moment in Moses's life, when he receives the call to take on the task of liberating the Israelites, why does God appear to him in this particular way? One of the participants offered an answer that I have never forgotten: "Because," he said, "to take this on, you have to have a fire burning within, an anger about injustice, a passion for the work of liberation. But that fire can overwhelm and consume you." *Burnout* is an all-too-common trait of those who do the work of social change. A bush that is aflame yet not consumed by the fire becomes a powerful metaphor for the godly work of Liberation that Moses is about to begin.

The Consuming Fire

I have had an immediate, visceral sense of being in God's presence very few times in my life. One such time occurred a few years after my father died. I had gone to a local synagogue for the daily evening prayer on the anniversary of his death. I was in a small group of people whom I mostly did not know, participating in a simple, fairly perfunctory service. All of which to say, I wasn't expecting anything out of the ordinary to occur. During the standing silent prayer, I was suddenly struck by an intense feeling of being literally in God's presence. I was terrified. I felt as if I were facing Something that held my life in Its hands, a Power that could end my life at any moment. I stood, and I breathed, and I wondered what would happen next. Traditionally, one ends the standing prayer by taking three steps backward and then sitting down. How could I possibly back away from the Source of Life and Death? I worried that I'd be standing in this small chapel for the rest of my life. After a few minutes, the intensity lessened, and I was able to walk three steps back and take my seat.

That experience taught me what the ancients knew only too well: that life is precarious and beyond our control, and that this awareness is part of what it means to know God. I glimpsed this truth for a few minutes that evening in a profound and visceral way. It's not an awareness that I can—or would want to—walk around with every day. Yet I don't regret having experienced it. To feel myself in YHVH's presence was powerful and beautiful as well as terrifying. This is the true meaning of the word *awe:* not just "Wow!" but also "Yikes!" It is this experience of the divine that the Torah seeks to capture when it calls God *"a consuming fire."*[4] There is something frightening and dangerous, as well as fascinating and mysterious, that is fundamental to the metaphor of God as fire.

At the burning bush, once he realizes that YHVH is speaking to him, Moses hides his face *"for he was afraid to look at God."*[5] When the Israelites encounter God at Mount Sinai, the Torah emphasizes the people's fear when they hear the divine voice speaking "out of the fire" on the mountain: *"Let us not die, then,"* they say, *"for this great fire will consume us!"*[6] Later in the Torah, we read a story about Aaron's sons Nadav and Avihu, who are priests in charge of the Mishkan, the portable sanctuary in the wilderness. For some reason, Nadav and Avihu make an unauthorized offering at the altar of the Mishkan. Suddenly, *"a fire came forth from YHVH and consumed them, and they died before YHVH."*[7] There is much debate about what, if anything, Nadav and Avihu did wrong. Whatever the explanation, the main point of the story seems to be that any misstep when in God's presence can mean being swallowed up by the divine Fire.

While almost anything can be dangerous in excess, the distance between warming your hands by a fire and singeing your fingers is a matter of inches. Fire is essential to human civilization, whether as a source of heat or a means of cooking food. The Torah itself is described by the early rabbis as "black fire written on white fire." Yet alongside its vital, life-giving aspects, the destructive power of fire is ever-present. Fire as warmth, light, and protection, and Fire as that which annihilates: the complex nature of this metaphor invites us to explore some of the most fraught and challenging aspects of experiencing the Divine.

Holy Fire, Holy Anger

Throughout the Hebrew Bible, God's anger manifests as fire. Indeed, all of the biblical words associated with divine anger are related in some way to heat. This is not surprising, as physical heat shows up as a metaphor for anger in many languages, including English—which is why we say someone is "steaming mad" or has a "fiery temper." God's anger is first described as a consuming fire in the episode of the golden calf. Furious that the Israelites have made an idol while awaiting Moses's return from Mount Sinai, YHVH says to him: "*I see that this is a stiff-necked people. Now, let Me be, that My anger may blaze forth against them and I will consume them, and make of you a great nation.*"[8] In this instance, Moses is able to talk God out of destroying the Israelites. But as the people continue to complain and rebel during their desert wanderings, the destructive power of divine Fire is unleashed time and again, "consuming" complainers and rebels alike.[9]

YHVH as "*a consuming fire*" is also called "*El qannā*"—a divine name that is usually translated "a jealous God." The word *qannā* often appears in the Hebrew Bible in conjunction with both God's anger and divine Fire, as in this verse from Psalm 79:

> *How long, YHVH? Will you be angry forever? How long will your qannā burn like fire?*[10]

In the human realm, the word *qannā* does indeed mean "jealousy." And in assuming that the primary biblical metaphor for God is a Big Person, many readers have understood *qannā* as a heated divine emotion. The end of the verse I just quoted is usually translated: "How long will your jealousy burn like fire?" This understanding has played a significant role in the unfortunate characterization of the "Old Testament God" as an angry, jealous old man.

One scholar, however, has made an argument for a very different way of understanding the divine *qannā,* one which aligns much better with the metaphor of God as Fire. Nissim Amzallag of Ben-Gurion University posits that *qannā* is not a divine version of jealousy but is rather an "essential attribute of YHVH" that is likened to the intense heat, fire, and lava flows of volcanoes.[11] All of these images are connected, he suggests, to the ancient metallurgical process of "furnace remelting." In this process, a corroded copper object was completely melted down in a furnace, and the molten metal was then shaped into something new. In the ancient world, it was not uncommon for divine beings to be associated with metallurgy, with the intense, transformative power of flame and heat. Amzallag concludes:

> [The] divine *qannā* was not viewed by the Israelites simply as the destructive expression of anger by God. Precisely as in furnace remelting, it was conceived as a wonder leading to a complete rejuvenation of creation through a massive destruction of shape.[12]

Divine *qannā* as a power akin to "furnace remelting" is both destructive *and* creative, completely reshaping one thing into another. How might understanding *qannā* as "furnace remelting" give us insight into biblical texts about divine anger and God's consuming fire?

In the Hebrew Bible, divine anger is directed at those who fail to align with God's ritual and ethical demands, which are intended for the betterment of humanity. God has plans for us, and gets frustrated when we deny those plans. The first time that God gets angry in the Torah is, somewhat surprisingly, in the encounter with Moses at the burning bush. After hearing God's message for him, Moses resists mightily the call to return to Egypt and free the Israelites. "Who am I to do such a thing?" he asks. He protests that the Israelites will never believe that he's actually on a mission from God, and besides, he's not much of a public speaker. After receiving reassurance after reassurance, Moses finally says, "Please, my lord, send somebody else!" Finally, "*YHVH's anger was kindled at Moses,*" and God tells him that it's time to go.[13]

Just as Moses kindles the divine anger by refusing the mission to free the oppressed Israelites, the newly freed slaves are warned that they too will suffer that anger if they fail to care for the most vulnerable in their midst. As they enter into the covenant at Sinai, YHVH tells the Israelites: "*You shall not oppress any widow or orphan. If you oppress them, when they cry out to me, I will surely hear their cry, and my anger shall burn hot.*"[14]

In the book of Numbers, which recounts the Israelites' forty years of wandering in the wilderness, God's "consuming fire" is unleashed when there is discord within the Israelite community. Complainers and rebels are consumed by divine fire when they refuse to accept the challenge of creating a new kind of society. When the covenant is denied, when God's plans are thwarted, when the people resist their destiny and try to turn back to what they left behind in Egypt—at those moments, the flames of divine anger blaze.

In prophetic texts, God's anger and the divine *qannā* are connected both to condemnation of oppressors and to a vision of transformation. The prophet Ezekiel declares that YHVH has spoken "*in the fire of my qannā*" against the nations that destroyed Jerusalem and exiled the Israelites, but it is also by the power of "*My qannā and My hot anger*" that YHVH will return the exiles to their land.[15] Similarly, the prophet Isaiah rails against injustice and corruption among the leaders in Jerusalem, foretelling fiery destruction and then the coming of a new king, who will reestablish the throne of the Davidic line "*in justice and righteousness.*" And all of this, the prophet declares, "*will be done by the qannā of YHVH.*"[16]

I first studied these texts about the fiery divine *qannā* with my congregants in June 2020, as protests in the aftermath of the murder of George Floyd were erupting in cities across America. A holy anger, accompanied by actual fire, blazed in those protests. Like the consuming fire of YHVH, once the fires of the protests were unleashed, they could not be easily controlled. The fires destroyed not just symbols of power like police stations but also neighborhood stores and institutions. An editorial in *The Economist* invoking James Baldwin's 1963 book *The Fire Next Time* noted:

> The fire this time is burning for the same reasons it has so often in the past: that many African-Americans still live in places with the worst schools, the worst health care and the worst jobs; that the rules apply differently to black people; the fact, rammed home by [COVID]-19, that whenever America suffers misfortune, black America suffers most; a sense that the police are there to keep a lid on a city's poor, even as they protect wealthy suburbs.[17]

Jeneé Osterheldt, a columnist with *The Boston Globe,* shared her own sorrow and anger with metaphors of fire a few days after the protests had started:

> A Minneapolis precinct was on fire. But I saw my people in the flames. George Floyd was killed Monday and no one was arrested. And they want me to care about that burning building with not one officer in it. You can rebuild a station. There is no resurrection for the dead Black bodies.

Osterheldt went on to note that the officer who had killed Floyd was not arrested until "the city blazed." She continued: "I hate that the livelihood of business owners is burning. But so are Black lives. And we know America's love language is money. So when lost profits mount, maybe leaders will look at the hate they give us and reconsider . . . America doesn't listen—not when you have Black skin. But you hear the fire because the heat is loud and the sparks are catching."[18]

As the Black Lives Matter movement swept across America and racial attitudes among many white people dramatically shifted, I thought about YHVH's fiery anger and the power of the divine *qannā*. Perhaps, as in the prophetic visions, there are times when profound injustice brings in its wake turmoil and destruction. Collective anger at injustice, like the flames that erupt when YHVH is angry, can get out of control. Yet out of those flames can also come disruptive and necessary transformation. As the calls to redress hundreds of years of injustice against Black and Native American people light a powerful fire in the hearts and minds of so many Americans, this next period in our nation's history will reveal if a true "remelting" is occurring, one in which the structures and ideologies of racism will be melted down so that something new and better, something truly wondrous, can emerge.

Qannā Awareness

As we studied biblical texts about the divine *qannā*, I asked my congregants to reflect on whether they had ever had a personal "furnace remelting" experience. I invited them to write about a difficult event in their lives that had led them to a new perspective or awareness. Are we ever seared by life—by loss, by failure—and some positive transformation or "reshaping" results?

One congregant wrote about the crushing experience of divorce and the years following in which she reinvented herself:

> From that divorce that I literally thought might destroy me, I feel like I am a phoenix that has grown out of the ashes, and am deeply grateful for the support and love I have had along the way, and the opportunities that life presents when one is open to them.

Another person wrote about the death of her beloved father and how she discovered a new perspective in its aftermath:

> The reality of our time, of our love, was still so incontestably real that I had to change my sense of what is

real in a world of life and death; I had to expand it to include his dying. Not that the loss, the leaving and being left, isn't the truth, but that it's not the only truth. I found I could feel the reality of his continued presence, and more largely a different relationship between life and death. It felt like the world expanded in an essential way.*

These reflections speak to the possibility of what we might call *qannā awareness*, which entails a willingness to engage with our own pain and suffering in such a way that we can learn and grow from it. In a talk she gave in 1977 called "The Transformation of Silence into Language and Action," the author and activist Audre Lorde described her first encounter with cancer as just this kind of "furnace remelting" experience:

> In becoming forcibly and essentially aware of my mortality, and of what I wished and wanted for my life, however short it might be, priorities and omissions became strongly etched in a merciless light, and what I most regretted were my silences. Of what had I ever been afraid? To question or to speak as I believed could have meant

---

* With thanks to Lisa Schneier for sharing this beautiful reflection.

pain, or death. But we all hurt in so many different ways, all the time, and pain will either change or end. Death, on the other hand, is the final silence. And that might be coming quickly, now, without regard for whether I had ever spoken what needed to be said, or had only betrayed myself into small silences, while I planned someday to speak, or waited for someone else's words. And I began to recognize a source of power within myself that comes from the knowledge that while it is most desirable not to be afraid, learning to put fear into a perspective gave me great strength.[19]

The "source of power" that Lorde discovered within herself was a sacred fire, kindled in the awareness of her own mortality, which gave her a new ability to speak her truth. In all of these reflections, I see the divine *qannā* at work, the transformative power that can emerge out of the fires of loss and fear. Like God speaking to the Israelites "out of the fire" at Sinai, there are times in our lives when we have the opportunity to hear a divine message coming directly out of our terror, our pain, if we are able to withstand it.

Tending the Fire of the Heart

Holy fire is not only that which descends from the heavens. There is power in lighting candles and tending to sacred fire, from the candles on birthday cakes to votive candles in churches to the ritual fires of Hindu Yajna and Native American ceremonies. In the Temple in Jerusalem a few thousand years ago, sacred fire was a central component of the priestly rituals. The Israelites brought sacrifices to be burnt on the altar during pilgrimage festivals, to atone for wrongdoing, to express gratitude, or simply as an act of devotion. Part of the job of the priests was to make sure a fire was always burning on the altar:

> *The fire on the altar shall be kept burning, not to go out: every morning the priest shall feed wood to it, lay out the burnt offering on it, and turn into smoke the fat parts of the offerings of well-being. A perpetual fire shall be kept burning on the altar, not to go out.*[20]

Some scholars suggest that the fire burning on the altar was intended to be an ever-present symbol of the godly Fire that appeared to the Israelites at Sinai. And the biblical word usually translated as "sacrifice" actually comes from a root meaning to "come close." The offerings that were burned on the altar were a way for the Israelites to connect to YHVH via their own, humanly created fire. The flames on the altar were both a reminder of God as Fire and a means of connecting to the divine.

When the Temple in Jerusalem was destroyed by the Roman army in the year 70 C.E., and along with it the priestly rituals that had been at the center of Israelite religion for over a thousand years, the sacrifices took on metaphorical meaning. In rabbinic tradition, the worship service of the Temple was transformed into "service of the heart"—which, for the rabbis, meant fixed daily prayer, set at the times of day of the erstwhile priestly offerings.

Expanding on this idea of prayer as akin to an offering on the altar, the Hasidic master Rabbi Zev Wolf of Zhitomyr taught:

> Do not think that the words of prayer as you say them go up to God. It is not the words themselves that ascend; it is rather the burning desire of your heart that rises like smoke toward heaven. If your prayer consists only of words and letters, and does not contain your heart's desire—how can it rise up to God?[21]

Rabbi Wolf's teaching suggests that true "service of the heart" is more than the words we say or the actions that we do. It is an offering of the self, of the "burning desire of the heart." "Service of the heart" does not mean only formal prayer. It can be any "service" I undertake that connects me to That which is Godly. To take on this type of service, I must, first, understand what the burning desire of my heart *is,* and then offer that to God, to the world, for the sake of healing and transformation.

There are many potential obstacles to discerning our holy "burning desire." In a culture that does its best to convince us that our deepest desires are for physical things—a new car or pair of shoes, the latest phone or TV, a better body or nicer house—it is not always so easy to locate our desire for something more lasting and meaningful. Some of us get the message that our own deepest desire is unimportant, that we are only meant to attend to the needs of others. It is also possible to get so worn down by the world that the burning desire of our heart feels as if it died out long ago.

What is amazing about embers, however, is that they can be banked for a long time, and then, with a bit of attention and gentle care, spark a new fire. Rabbi Yehudah Leib of Ger taught that when the Torah says that the fire on the altar "will not go out," this is not only a command but also a promise.[22] The fire perpetually burning on the altar is a reminder that the metaphorical flame in the human heart never actually goes out. We just need to find it, and tend it, in order for that inner flame to burn true.

In his reflection on the path to finding our particular service in this world, the theologian Frederick Buechner writes that "the place God calls you to is the place where your deep gladness and the world's deep hunger meet."[23] I think of this "deep gladness" as that inner flame, the burning desire of our hearts for that which will give our lives meaning and bring us true happiness. To discern my "deep gladness" does not mean being self-centered, or excusing myself from responsibility for others. To be a vessel for godliness in this world, to meet the "world's deep hunger," I need to know what it is that feeds my heart and my soul, and then, like the priest at the altar, I need to bring the wood to keep those fires burning.

God as Fire Practice

Fire Meditation

As I discovered on my first retreat experience, watching fire is a very natural form of meditation. Many spiritual traditions include gazing at a candle as a formal practice.[24] Meditating on the flames of a fire or a candle is a wonderful technique for calming the mind, as well as an opportunity to experience the association of the divine with fire. Here are a few ways to do this practice:

- Light a candle in a dark room, and find a place to sit in front of it, a foot or two away. For ten or fifteen minutes, focus your gaze on the flame of the candle. As with any meditation, your attention will wander; when you notice that this has happened, gently bring your awareness back to the candle. Notice colors and movement in the flame. See what changes, and what remains the same. Breathe in a relaxed way as you watch. This can be a lovely way to calm the mind in the evening (and shift your focus from screens) before heading to bed.

- You can do something similar either with an actual fire, in a fireplace or firepit, or you can find a video of a fireplace or campfire online (there are many available! Some show a fire burning in real time, instead of an endless loop of just a few minutes of an actual fire). Once the fire is burning (or you've started the video), do as you would with the candle: sit in a relaxed yet alert position, and watch the flames. As much as you can, let the sight and sound of the fire fill your mind. See what you notice, and gently bring your attention back to the fire when your mind wanders.

Whether you are gazing at a fire or a candle, see what happens if you imagine God's presence within the flame. This can be especially powerful to do if you are experiencing difficulty or sadness. Imagine that God is right there, in the fire of the pain, calling to you. If you are able to feel the warmth of the fire, take that in. If the fire or flame feels like a comforting presence, welcome that as well. Just as the column of fire guided the Israelites on their journey, see where this visual meditation takes you.

Working with Anger

As we saw in the biblical texts about God's anger, there are times when a "holy fire" of anger is an appropriate, even sacred response to events in our lives or in the world around us. Anger is a completely normal—and healthy— reaction to situations of abuse or oppression. Anger is like a warning bell in our nervous systems, letting us know that something is wrong and needs attention. To get ourselves out of an abusive situation, we may need to first realize that we are angry.

Yet anger, like fire, can also be profoundly destructive. It can overwhelm us, causing us to act in damaging ways either to ourselves or others. It can consume our spirits and destroy our relationships. Often, anger covers over emotions like fear or sadness, and prevents us from attending to a deeper level of pain. It is also true that there is no universal experience of anger, because we are socialized in very different ways—depending on our gender, our race, our cultural background—in how or even if we should feel anger. Because anger, like fire, is both necessary and powerful, it is important that we become aware of how it operates within us, and learn how we might channel it in productive ways.

Anger for the Sake of Heaven: One of the founders of Hasidic Judaism, Dov Baer of Mezeritch, taught:

> Your anger should always be "for the sake of heaven." Direct your anger toward the forces of evil in the person who upsets you, and not at the person himself. Understand that these forces scare him into doing evil things. Then you can use your anger to bring these forces under the sway of holiness.[25]

In rabbinic tradition, the phrase "for the sake of heaven" refers to something undertaken for the purpose of reaching a higher truth, rather than self-aggrandizement or an ulterior motive. Dov Baer suggests that we can consciously use our anger for a higher purpose.

Anger "for the sake of heaven" is anger that I can channel in such a way that it becomes transformative—both for myself and for the world around me. As I was writing this chapter, I read an interview with the African American hip-hop artist Oompa. When asked how she was interacting with the movement for Black lives, she responded, "What I will say is that I live in a constant state of rage about being Black. You know? I'm happy that other people have been ignited . . . But I think that my rage isn't new. I've learned to live with this rage—or this understanding, or this sadness—of what it means to be Black in America." She went on to describe her artistic practice as both a reflection on her state of being and a vehicle for catharsis.[26] Turning a "constant state of rage" into art is a powerful example of "anger for the sake of heaven," as something transformative that seeks to bring the forces of evil "under the sway of holiness." We can turn a burning rage into art, into creative protest, in service of reshaping our society.

To use our anger in this holy way, according to Dov Baer, we need to be clear about the true target of our anger. It is not the essence of the person or people who have angered us. Rather, the target is either a particular behavior that needs to be addressed, or a greater evil that the difficult person's words or actions represent. Dr. Martin Luther King Jr. taught something similar when he made clear that his enemy was racism, not the racist individuals he encountered.

Using our anger to bring "evil forces under the sway of holiness" is a reminder that the ultimate goal is to completely transform something that is destructive into something that is holy, whether a problematic personal behavior or an oppressive situation. It is not to destroy another person (even if imagining that might feel good). My anger at the "evil forces" becomes a motivation for healing, for myself and others. Even asking the question "How can I bring the negative forces I am facing under the sway of holiness?" can help transform an angry feeling into a productive force for transformation.

To be able to discern whether or not my anger is merely self-serving or is indeed "for the sake of heaven," I need to be able to step back, to take a breath, to settle my body and my mind. When the warning bell of anger goes off, I need to ask myself: What is really making me angry? If my anger is "for the sake of heaven," it means that I am truly concerned about a wrong that is being done, either to myself or to others. If it is "not for the sake of heaven," it may mean that I am simply frustrated that I can't have my way, or my ego is wounded.

To be able to discern the nature of my anger, I need to take time before I respond. I also need to trust that "anger for the sake of heaven" will not dissipate, and as long as it is not an emergency situation, I can address the cause of my anger after I have had time to chart the best course of action. In contrast, defensive, self-involved anger will disappear if I can get a little space from it and not feed the fire.

The Match and the Fuse: The negative form of anger, the kind that can consume us for no higher purpose, is that which emerges from impatience and frustration and a desire for control. It can also be an unconscious reaction to something that we perceive as a threat that is not a true source of danger. Anger can become our default reaction to any situation in which we expect things to be easier, faster, or simply different from what they are. Other people become obstacles to having things go our way, and we get angry.

In these situations we need to cultivate, in the words of the Mussar teacher Alan Morinis, the ability to "open the space between the match and the fuse."[27] We can't necessarily stop ourselves from feeling angry, but we can learn to pause before saying or doing something that will be hurtful to ourselves or others. In that pause, we can decide whether the fuse needs to be lit or whether we should blow out the match. One of the easiest ways to accomplish this is to remember to breathe, slowly and mindfully, when anger arises. Even a few conscious breaths can create enough space to keep ourselves from doing something we might regret.

We can also turn our attention from the object of our anger to our bodies. Ask yourself: Where is the anger? See if you can feel it—perhaps in your belly, or chest, or throat. Breathe gently into that area. Don't push the sensations away; rather, explore them with a gentle curiosity. By shifting your attention from the story about the anger—which tends to fuel the fire—and toward the sensations of the body, you can further expand the space between the match and the fuse. Feelings of anger are usually accompanied by a very convincing story about why our anger is righteous and justified. To be able to tell if that story is true or not, the fire will need to cool a bit.

From Scarcity to Gratitude: Rabbi Zelig Pliskin[28] teaches that another root cause of anger is a perception of scarcity, of there just not being enough. In these situations, practicing gratitude is a powerful antidote to destructive anger. For example, I tend to get angry when I am driving, especially if I haven't left myself enough time to get from point A to point B. When I am focused on the lack of time to get where I need to go, anger arises at anything that exacerbates that perceived lack—which is usually a car in front of me going slower than I'd like. When this happens,

I find it helpful to shift my focus from what I lack to what I have. Instead of focusing on my lack of time, I can be grateful that I have a car. Sometimes, when I'm driving to synagogue on a Shabbat morning and I get stuck behind another car and am worried I'll be late, I pretend that the driver ahead of me is actually a Shabbat angel. This angel is driving slowly to remind me to take my foot off the gas, relax, and appreciate that it's Shabbat. I give thanks for the angel, and watch my anger dissipate.

Tending the Fire of the Heart

"Service of the heart" is that which connects us to the Godliness that fills all of creation. It can happen in many realms, from working for social change to fostering loving relationships to creating spiritual community or caring for the earth. It might take the form of teaching or studying, making music or writing poetry, protesting or praying. And just as the priests in the Temple had to work to keep a fire burning on the altar, so we need to pay attention to the inner fire that fuels our service.

The Torah relates that each morning, one of the priests would remove the ashes of the previous day's burnt offering from the altar, and then take the ashes to a ritually pure place outside the camp. Then he would add new wood to the fire, to make sure that it never went out.[29] We can understand these instructions as an invitation to explore what feeds the fire—the passion, the inspiration, the "deep gladness"—within our hearts, and what accumulates to smother those flames.

Clearing Out the Ashes: Often, the obstacles to fulfilling the service of our hearts come from within ourselves. We get stuck in old patterns, or lose track of what is truly meaningful. We get burned out, unable to feel any passion for our work in the world. If we've had a significant loss, we can become mired in despair, unable to find the inner flame that once gave us joy. Inner obstacles to making needed changes in our lives can include habits of thought or action. Here is a practice to identify and begin to release the obstacles in your heart:

- Tear or cut up a piece of paper into slips. On each one, write down a habit, a mind-state or an old story that is holding you back in some way. It might be a tendency toward judging yourself or others harshly. It might be all the can'ts and shouldn'ts that you've told yourself. It might be a habit of unnecessary anger, or arrogance, or laziness. It might be a fear of change, or an attachment to an unhealthy craving. It might be a fantasy you've been unwilling to let go. Be honest with yourself, and know that none of these things define you—they are simply accumulations of old patterns, like the remains of old offerings on the altar.

- Place the slips of paper into a large, fireproof bowl. Take a moment to affirm your intention to offer it up and let it all go. Give it to God, the holy consuming Fire. Light the paper on fire, and watch it burn. Once it has burned up, be mindful about removing the ashes—you can bury them outdoors, or place them in the trash, or wash them away. As you do so, allow yourself to see that the old ashes are truly gone.

Feeding the Fire: It is important to pay attention to what feeds the fire in our hearts. You might be aware of what nourishes you in a deep way, and you just need to make sure you make time and space for it—whether it's being in nature or connecting with good friends, practicing yoga or meditation, making music or art or delicious food. This can be a challenge for anyone who has time-consuming obligations. But even if you are caring for young kids or elderly parents or working long hours, see if you can carve out some time each week for at least one soul-nourishing activity. Sometimes we let care for our spirits drop to the very bottom of our to-do list. Notice if you can at least listen to music you love on the way to work, or do meditation with your kids, or make time to connect with friends.

Just like the priest schlepping the wood to the altar every morning, feeding our inner fire can sometimes feel like a chore. It might not be the easiest or most available thing to do. It can be helpful to make a chart of soul-feeding practices, and keep it somewhere you can see. Write down all of the things you know nourish you, and keep track of when you do them. You might decide that some need to be daily practices, or weekly, or once a month. Be realistic, and keep track of how you are doing. Be sure to celebrate when you nourish yourself regularly!

If you're not sure what feeds your soul, start paying attention to what contributes to a sense of well-being or joy. I sometimes go for a hike and only then realize how much I have missed being in nature. If you spend time with a variety of people, notice how you feel after interacting with them, and see if some leave you feeling more energized or better about yourself than others. If you haven't checked out formal spiritual practices, try out something new and see if it helps you feel balanced or sustained— yoga or meditation or tai chi are good places to start. Take an art or dance class and see what happens, or choose music to listen to that is calming and uplifting. I once played

Bach in my car instead of listening to the news every day for a month, and it had a profoundly positive effect on my mood. Notice what energizes you and what exhausts you, and you will start to learn what is the fuel for your own sacred fire.

BECOMING

O ne of my favorite TV shows when I was a kid was *My Favorite Martian,* a sitcom from the 1960s. Ray Walston played a Martian anthropologist who crash-landed in America and was taken in by a newspaper reporter. While I recall very little of what exactly happened on the show, I have two distinct memories of the Martian, whom the reporter pretends is his "Uncle Martin" to hide his true identity. Uncle Martin had two retractable antennae at the back of his head, and he could levitate things by pointing his index finger at them.

I really, really wanted to be able to do that. I would sit in the bathroom (presumably so as to pursue this goal in private), point my finger at random objects, and concentrate really hard. I mean really hard. Not surprisingly, I was unsuccessful in my levitation attempts. But I kept trying!

Why have I held on to this odd memory? I think because I like what it says about my eight-year-old self, trying to achieve a superpower by the sheer dint of my will. It was a memory that came to me as I reflected on the human capacity for change and transformation. What is possible, and what is not? And how do we reflect the *tzelem Elohim*, the divine image, in this process?

The Source of Novelty

As wind / As water / As fire / As life / God is both creative and destructive / Demanding and Yielding / Sculptor and clay. God is Infinite Potential: God is Change

—*Octavia Butler*[1]

In the early twentieth century, the mathematician and philosopher Alfred North Whitehead posited an intriguing new way to think about the nature of reality. Whitehead's lifetime (1861–1947) spanned a momentous period in the history of science. Charles Darwin's *On the Origin of Species* had been published at the end of 1859, bringing to popular attention the emerging field of evolutionary biology. By the early twentieth century, theoretical physicists had proven that energy and matter are interchangeable, and that the most fundamental building blocks of the universe can act as both particles and waves. Taken together, these scientific revolutions suggested a dynamic, ever-changing physical world, from the realm of quarks and electrons on up to human beings.

In alignment with these new understandings, Whitehead argued that everything that is alive (what he called "actual") is always in process and is constantly being made anew. Even more, everything that is alive is itself a process. Whitehead described physical reality as not being made up of little units of matter, but rather moments of becoming, what he called "drops of experience." From elementary particles through the most complex life-forms, all living beings are a succession of "drops of experience."

How does this process of becoming work? Whitehead emphasized that each moment is not predetermined; there are many possibilities for what comes next. Every form of life incorporates two things, in every moment: the preceding experience of that which came before, and the element of novelty, of something creative and new. From moment to moment, each living process interacts with its environment, is affected by that interaction, and is no longer what it was before. Each moment of our existence is not exactly like the moment that came before, and neither are we.[2]

This is all sort of abstract, but if I think of myself now

versus eight-year-old me, I can see the process that White-head describes. On the one hand, I have a sense of continuity with my younger self; I have no doubt that it was actually me, sitting in the bathroom, pointing my finger at my toothbrush. And yet the physical truth is that the vast majority of the cells in my body die off at regular intervals and are replaced. My bones, blood, organs, skin, and hair are not composed of the same cells as the me of a decade ago, much less fifty years ago. Besides the natural changes in my body that have come with age, I've also witnessed some pretty substantial changes in my persona over the years. When I was eight, I had no idea I would become a lesbian or a rabbi. I've become more even-keeled over the years, I've deepened my sense of spiritual connection, and I've completely lost the ability to write songs like I could in my teens and twenties.

But my sense of personal continuity is not completely imaginary. Some parts of my brain are the same as youthful me, and the DNA that programs my cells hasn't changed over my lifetime. The "what came before" is that which makes adult me have some relation to eight-year-old me, and it ensures that I will never become a frog or a sunflower (or a television Martian). The "something new," the component of novelty, is that which has caused me to steadily change and grow.

Interestingly, Whitehead started out as an atheist, but over time he became convinced that for the universe to function in the way that he understood it, there had to be something that he ultimately identified as God. For Whitehead, God was the answer to the question: If there are possibilities for becoming that have not yet existed, where does that possibility come from? In his introduction to Whitehead's thought, C. Robert Mesle writes:

> Every event in the world, every momentary drop of experience, begins with a two-fold experience of God and the past actual world . . . Whitehead was convinced that, if there were only the world, there could be no *new* possibilities, nothing that had not already been done. If that were the case, the world could only repeat itself. There must be something actual, in addition to the past world, that acts as the source of genuine novelty.[3]

Whitehead concluded that God is the "source of genuine novelty." Even more, God shares in this capacity for newness, and is Itself in process. As all living beings interact with the divine source of novelty, God too changes, ever evolving along with us.

While it may seem rather obvious that our physical reality consists of constant change and evolution, this has not been the case when it comes to thinking about the divine. For millennia, theologians have assumed that God's nature is radically different from the world God created. We might change, but God does not. Indeed, following the Greek philosopher Plato, much of Jewish, Muslim, and Christian theology has assumed that God's "perfection" lies in God being unchanging (because any change in God would imply that there was something less than perfect that needed to change). Whitehead's insights, and the school of thought he inspired called *process theology*, make the opposite argument. As the Source of newness in the universe, the essence of divinity is to change and grow.

For our purposes, we do not have to decide whether these ideas of Whitehead's are objectively "true" or not. What his philosophy does offer us is an invitation to move beyond thinking about God as a "being" of any sort, and to instead encounter God in the metaphors of Process and Potential.

Ehyeh

A few thousand years before Whitehead, the authors of the Torah came up with their own version of the divine Process. Back at the burning bush, as Moses tries to argue his way out of going back to Egypt to free the Hebrew slaves, he asks two important questions. The first is:

Who am I, that I should go to Pharaoh and free the Israelites from Egypt?

God's response is not what you would expect. Instead of reassuring Moses that he has lots of great leadership qualities, God replies: "*I will be with you.*" We'll come back to that answer in a moment. Moses is not convinced, and tries a new question:

When I come to the Israelites and say to them, "the God of your ancestors has sent me," and they say to me, "What is Its name?"—what should I say to them?

God's response here is mysterious and beautiful: "*God said to Moses, 'Ehyeh-Asher-Ehyeh,' and said, 'Thus you shall say to the Israelites, 'Ehyeh sent me to you.'"*[4]

The phrase offered to Moses as the divine Name—*Ehyeh Asher Ehyeh*—can most literally be translated as "I will be that I will be," or "I am Becoming That I am Becoming." The word *Ehyeh* is the first-person future tense of the verb *to be*. It is this shortened name, *Ehyeh*, that Moses is instructed to use to let the Israelites know Who, or What, has sent him to them. It is as if Moses is to say to his enslaved kin: "There is a Power in the universe Whose name is Becoming. What is now is not what will be in the future. This Power of transformation will free you from slavery, because It makes possible the most audacious change."

This was the message that God was trying to give Moses in response to his first question, "Who am I to go to Pharaoh?" There, he received the answer: "*Ehyeh* will be with you." When Moses first encounters the divine, he is entirely unprepared for the call to liberate the Israelites. He lacks confidence, and worries that he doesn't have all the answers. God tells him that that's okay. *Ehyeh* will be with him, and he will become what he needs to become.

In this encounter, Moses is introduced to God not as a supernatural being but as the Process of Becoming. *Ehyeh* is the biblical name for Whitehead's source of novelty. In the words of process theologian Charles Hartshorne, God represents "a maximum of potentiality, of unactualized power to be."[5] *Ehyeh* is That which makes transformation not just possible but necessary.

If God is the ultimate potentiality of all potentialities, then change is godly. Perfection does not lie in achieving some final state of completeness. In fact, such a state is impossible. Change, development, evolution, are not just natural aspects of material reality—they are its most godly aspects. In the words of visionary science fiction writer Octavia Butler: "God is Infinite Potential; God is Change."

God's Learning Curve

With a divine name like "I am Becoming," it is not surprising that the Torah depicts God as continually learning and growing. In the beginning, YHVH sees all of Creation and says, "It is good!" But as soon as human beings are created, they start doing surprising things, like ignoring divine instructions and then killing each other. God learns a lot about humanity in the first chapters of Genesis, and by chapter 6 regrets ever having made them. Far from being "all-knowing," in the sense of already knowing all that is and will ever be, YHVH is continually surprised and confounded by human behavior, and keeps needing to adapt.

God's learning curve, in the biblical imagination, is made necessary by humanity's freedom to make choices (and our tendency to make bad ones). In the second chapter of Genesis, the first humans are given a choice: to follow instructions and refrain from eating the fruit of the Tree of Knowledge of Good and Evil, or not. They choose to eat, are ejected from the Garden of Eden, and so begins the biblical version of human history, with all of its ups and downs.

At the very end of the Torah, in the book of Deuteronomy, Moses faces the entire Israelite community as they stand on the border of the promised land. He exhorts them to follow the path of loving God and keeping the covenant, and emphasizes that ultimately, their fate is up to them:

> *I call heaven and earth to witness for you this day: I have put before you life and death, blessing and curse. Choose life—so that you and your children may live.*[6]

The Torah begins and ends with a choice. The first choice: to become human adults, with the ability to know right from wrong and do good or bad, or to remain infant-like, innocent and incapable of doing harm, forever. The second choice: to accept a path of covenantal obligation, in order to create a holy community in relationship with the Source of Life, or to reject that path.

In the Torah's telling, the first choice was made for us by Adam and Eve. We are mortal beings with free will, able to distinguish and choose between good and evil. The second choice, however, comes in a passage in which Moses tells the Israelites, "You are standing here *today*." We as readers are to imagine ourselves in our very own "today," confronted with the choice between blessing and curse, life and death.

Who wouldn't choose the path of blessing and of life? Unfortunately, that question is all too often answered in the negative. The human embrace of ignorance and greed, the seeming death wish that drives us to put our selfish, short-term desires above the health of the planet on which we depend for our very lives, is sadly alive and well. The divine power of Becoming that lives in our cells and in our consciousness cannot guarantee that we will make the right choices.

There is a midrash, a rabbinic commentary on the biblical Creation story, that imagines God asking the angels whether human beings should be created. Half of the angels say yes, praising humanity's ability to do acts of love and justice. The other half say no, pointing out the human capacity for lies and violence. In the end, God goes ahead and makes Adam. This midrash illustrates a deep truth: that with the evolution of human beings, the potential for great goodness in the world was inevitably accompanied by the potential for great evil. From an amoeba to a fish to a human being, with every level of evolutionary complexity comes greater capacity for choice, and greater opportunity for love as well as hate, for creativity as well as destruction.

God as Becoming invites us to embrace the complexity and uncertainty that is at the heart of the evolutionary process. In another midrash, the rabbis imagine God creating and destroying 974 worlds before this one.[7] What a marvelous contrast to the philosophers' unchanging, all-knowing deity! I love the image of God making and then crumpling up 974 worlds in order to come up with the one we inhabit. The creative process—whether God's or our own—of necessity includes mistakes as well as successes, discovery along with destruction. To again quote Octavia Butler:

> God is Change
> And hidden within Change
> Is surprise, delight,
> Confusion, pain,
> Discovery, loss,
> Opportunity, and growth.[8]

Embracing Uncertainty

One winter at a retreat for Jewish clergy, I met Cantor Sue Knight Deutsch, who told a group of us an amazing story. Earlier that year, she found herself facing a life choice that terrified her. As she shared with me later, "It felt like I was jumping off a cliff. So I decided to embody and face my fear by actually jumping off a cliff." She decided to go paragliding. I listened in awe as Sue described the instructor's words to her: "Run toward the edge of the cliff, and when the ground disappears beneath your feet, keep running." Deeply fearful, she did as she was told. Stepping off the cliff into nothing, having faith in her instructor and the glider that held them both, she was aloft, getting a view of the world that she'd never had before.[9]

Cantor Sue's story is about facing our fears, but it's also about faith. Not blind faith—Sue had done her research and found an experienced paragliding instructor who had never had an accident. But as she wrote to me later about this experience: "The worst part of 'jumping' was running toward the edge of the cliff. In that moment when you hit the edge, have faith you will be lifted."

Too often, people misconstrue faith with certainty, assuming that to "have faith" means to be confident in the outcome, to know exactly where things are going to end up. But as life has a way of teaching us, we rarely know where we're going to end up, or how we're going to get there. Martin Luther King Jr. is reported to have once said, "Faith is the first step, even when you don't see the whole staircase."[10] To take that first step, we have to trust the Process, while relinquishing our need to control where it might ultimately take us. As the Buddhist teacher Sharon Salzberg notes: "Any insistence that people or circumstances meet our exact expectations is not faith, but another effort at control, bound to end in disappointment."[11]

If we embrace God as Change, as Becoming, then we have to be willing to relinquish our need to be in control. Things as they are now—in our own lives, in the world around us—are often not what we expected. Things as they are now will inevitably change, in ways that we cannot predict.

The COVID-19 pandemic was a very profound (if very painful) teacher of this challenging truth, especially for those of us who take for granted a modicum of stability in our lives. On an individual level, it became difficult to plan more than a week or two ahead. As a society, we experienced things closing and then reopening and then closing up again. Constant adaptation became the theme of our lives. But even without major shocks to our systems, the truth is that we can never really predict the future. The sooner we learn to embrace the reality of uncertainty, the better off we will be in navigating the changes that will inevitably confront us.

But does embracing uncertainty mean stepping off a cliff? How do we know that there is something there to hold us up, to help us soar, when contemplating that much openness?

In her essay "Living in Radical Uncertainty," the science fiction author and critic Martha A. Bartter writes:

> So how can we manage to live in a world that keeps changing around us? For that matter, how can we manage to live with our own continually-changing selves? We must use our senses in a new way: to detect what goes on in and around us now, without expecting it to seem "the same" as it did before. We should approach life as a continual surprise, and remember that though some surprises feel unpleasant, some surprises please us immensely. (Assuming that "surprise" equals "bad" takes most of the fun out of living.)[12]

Some time in my forties, my spouse, Gina, organized a surprise birthday party for me. I thought that we were going to one of my favorite restaurants with our kids and my brother's family. About an hour before we were supposed to head out, people started mysteriously arriving at our house. First it was my nieces and nephew, telling me they'd decided to come down a little early. Then it was Gina's sister, saying she wanted to bring something by for me. Then it was a good friend, suggesting she was in the neighborhood for work and just wanted to come by and tell me, "Happy birthday." By the time the tenth person "dropped in," I finally realized what was up. It was a sneak surprise party!

The thing is, I am very bad at changing my expectations quickly. I was really looking forward to dinner at that restaurant. All of a sudden, I was in the midst of a birthday party I hadn't planned for. I never told Gina any of this, and it was a lovely evening, but I always felt a bit guilty that I wasn't as appreciative of her organizing this birthday gathering as I should have been. Now I wonder, if I had been practicing what Bartter preaches—living with an expectation of "continual surprise"—I might have enjoyed myself a lot more that night, and been far more appreciative of my loving spouse in that moment.

The reality that all we can really know is what is happening in this moment doesn't mean that we shouldn't make plans, just that we should do so with the full awareness that surprise might lie around the corner. And when that surprise does arrive, we can pause and, as Bartter suggests, pay attention to what is actually going on in that moment both inside and around us, before getting too grumpy or frustrated or blaming others for putting us in an unexpected position.

But what do we do about the longer-term challenges of continual change? How can we best navigate our uncertain and unsettling world? How do we channel the Power of Becoming in ways that are transformative—for the good, and not for creating more chaos—over the long haul?

The social justice activist and healer adrienne maree brown writes powerfully about "staying purposeful in the face of constant change," and the practice of what she calls "intentional adaptation":

> Change is definitely going to happen, no matter what we plan or expect or hope for or set in place. We will adapt to that change, or we will become irrelevant. But this element is not about pure adaptation . . . I am talking about the combination of adaptation with intention . . . This is the process of changing while staying in touch with our deeper purpose and longing.[13]

The practice of staying connected to our "deeper purpose and longing" as we navigate an ever-changing reality is about channeling the transformative power of *Ehyeh Asher Ehyeh*.

It is so easy to get caught up in the confusion and chaos that surround us. *Ehyeh* reminds us that in our work in the world, in our relationships, in our spiritual practice, we can become sacred vessels for the divine Potential that courses through each of us, one step at a time. We can do so having no idea where we will end up, but trusting in the Process that will get us there.

Making New Each Day

In the summer of 2002, nine coal miners were trapped for over three days in the flooded Quecreek Mine in western Pennsylvania. The situation was dire, and the men believed they were not going to make it. After they were rescued, one of the miners reported staying up all night despite his exhaustion, so that he could see "the miracle of the sunrise."

I think of that miner when I say the daily Jewish prayer *Yotzer Or,* which blesses God as That which "makes new each day the work of Creation." This prayer invites us to experience the world as if it is in fact made anew each day—to feel, as that miner felt, that each sunrise is a miracle. This mind-state—what we might call a sense of awe—is another component of finding faith in the face of uncertainty. In the words of Rabbi Abraham Joshua Heschel:

Awe is more than an emotion; it is a way of understanding. Awe is itself an act of insight into a meaning greater than ourselves . . . The meaning of awe is to realize that life takes place under wide horizons, horizons that range beyond the span of an individual life or even the life of a nation, a generation, or an era. Awe enables us to perceive in the world intimations of the divine, to sense in small things the beginning of infinite significance, to sense the ultimate in the simple.[14]

A sense of awe is a matter of perspective, a kind of re-framing of our daily experience. In traditional Jewish practice, we say this blessing three times a day: "We give thanks to YHVH, the Source of Life . . . for the miracles that greet us every day, each morning, noon, and night." Miracles that happen every morning, noon, and night! These clearly are not wondrous events outside the laws of nature. The blessing asks us to celebrate the "intimations of the divine" that Heschel describes finding in "small things"—the regular miracles of our breath and our bodies, our capacity to love, the beauty of nature, the reminders of all that is precious in life.

Cultivating a sense of awe, however, does not mean fooling ourselves into thinking things are fine when they are not. adrienne maree brown writes, "It is easy to think everything is a miracle during a moment of external joy . . . What is harder is to bring my miraculous perspective to grief, to injustice, to delayed travel, to broken technology, to conflict, to changes of plans, to mercury retrograde—things that can be filed under 'bad day' or 'bad life.'" brown teaches that we can examine our habitual reactions to change, and see if "those reactions create space for opportunity, possibility, and continuing to move towards [our] vision." We can "listen for the opportunity" in the seeming crisis or the uncertainty we are facing. She says: "I choose what to embody, what to long for, even as the horizon shifts before me. The adaptation is up to me."[15]

This "adaptation" is our capacity to channel the Power of Becoming, to become vessels for the ongoing Flow of divine creativity as we face the challenges and surprises that arise in our lives. The eighteenth-century Hasidic master Yaakov Yitzchak Rabinowicz of Peshischa taught that God as *Ehyeh* accompanies us in our work of personal transformation: "When a person says 'I will be good from today on,' God immediately responds to them: 'I will be (*Ehyeh*) with you, and my Presence will rest upon you.'"[16] God does not force us to change; we are not marionettes in a preordained puppet show. Rather, we share in the divine power of potentiality, and we can draw upon it as we seek to make change in our lives.

When we experience God as Infinite Potential, we affirm the divinity inherent in our own process of becoming. In that process, we seek to become the fullest, most powerful version of ourselves. I think that this was what I was aiming for, in a somewhat fanciful and misguided way, in my youthful attempts at levitation. I wanted to be more than I was. In the ensuing years, as I have worked to live into my values, to deepen my spiritual practice, to practice kindness, to do what I can to address injustice and foster covenantal community, I can feel a divine dynamic at play. There is no particular place at which I will arrive, no end point to this journey. Just a process, moment to moment, of living into the best aspects of myself.

Ehyeh Practices

Becoming New with Each Breath

There is an intimate connection between the biblical name YHVH—which is grammatically related to the name *Ehyeh*—and breathing. As Rabbi Arthur Green explains,

"All the letters that make up this name served in ancient Hebrew interchangeably as consonants and as vowels. Really they are mere vowels, mere breath."[17] Rabbi Green teaches that this holiest of divine names is more verb than noun. It is dynamic, in constant motion, just like the ongoing process of breathing in and breathing out.

Building on the rabbinic idea that YHVH creates the world anew each day, the eighteenth-century Hasidic master Levi Yitzchak of Berdichev teaches:

> We should constantly bring to mind that from moment to moment the blessed Creator, in great love and compassion, gives us new life force. From moment to moment the Creator makes us new . . . At each moment, the breath seeks to leave us, and the Blessed Holy One, with great compassion, does not let the breath depart. And so it is that when we bring this to mind continually, we are indeed created anew, from moment to moment.[18]

Rabbi Levi Yitzchak wants us to take seriously God as *Ehyeh*, and our own godly capacity for personal transformation. As he notes, this is something that doesn't just happen; it is an attitude that we need to cultivate, to continually "bring to mind." His teaching suggests that we can foster a moment-to-moment awareness of our potential in each moment, using our breath. Levi Yitzchak invites us to experience each in-breath as a gift of "new life force" from YHVH, to receive each moment as a new opportunity. With each breath, we can know that we are not stuck in what has been. We can simply appreciate the power of this moment, right here, and open to what might be next.

Y-H-V-H Meditation: To do this practice, sit in a comfortable position. Either close your eyes, or rest them with soft focus on a spot on the ground in front of you. Take a moment to notice your body, the sensation of sitting. Then, bring your attention to your breath. Without trying to breathe in any particular way, begin to notice each part of the process of breathing. Notice the pause before the in-breath. Notice the sensation of the lungs filling with air. Pay attention to the belly, the chest, the throat, as you breathe in. Then, notice the pause before the out-breath, and the sensation of breathing out. Then begin the process again. The mind will naturally wander, but when you notice that it has drifted away, gently bring it back to paying attention to the sensations of breathing in and breathing out.

Try experiencing each in-breath as a gift of love, or with an attitude of "continual surprise." Wow, I am breathing in! Notice it. Appreciate it. See how this breath is not exactly like the last breath you took. Say a small thanks as you start to inhale again.

If you'd like, you can invite YHVH into your breath practice. First, you'll need to know what the letters of this Hebrew name look like:

- The first letter is called *Yud,* and it's like a small point: י
- The second is called *Hay,* and it looks like this: ה
- The third letter is called *Vav,* and it looks like this: ו
- And the last letter is *Hay* again: ה

As you sit and pay attention to your breath, you can visualize the little point of the י in the pause before the in-breath. Then, visualize the first ה as your lungs fill with air. In the moment before the out-breath, visualize the straight line of the ו like an upright spine when the lungs are full. As you breathe out, visualize the second ה. You can use the letters as an anchor for your awareness, helping you keep your attention on each moment of the process of breathing in and breathing out. Feel the "verb-ness" of this holy name as it flows with your breath.

Blessing Daily Miracles

The Jewish blessings that acknowledge YHVH as the Power that renews creation and as the Source of daily miracles are intended to wake us up to the godliness that is manifest in every aspect of creation, even—or especially—when we're not feeling like things are so miraculous. One midrash goes so far as to claim that those who fail to say a blessing when they see the sun rise or set are as if they are dead, even while they are alive.[19]

That insight is bolstered by contemporary research in neuroscience, which suggests that practicing gratitude has a measurable positive effect on our physical health, our mental well-being, and our relationships. But even with this knowledge, not enough of us engage in daily gratitude practices. It is easy to start such a practice; the challenge is to maintain it! Here are a few possibilities:

Blessing the New Day: Each morning, recite the Jewish prayer of appreciation for the dawning of each new day. You might want to do this while out for a walk, or looking out the window at the world around you. Think of that Pennsylvania miner, receiving the sunrise as if it were a miracle. To emphasize the metaphor of God not as a static "thing" but an ongoing process, I have capitalized some of the verbs in this blessing to suggest that these might be "verb names" for the divine.[20] To vocalize "YHVH," you can say, "Adonai," or "Yah," or simply breathe. Here is my translation of the key themes of this prayer:

Blessed is the Source of Life, LIGHTING UP the earth and all that lives upon it, and with compassion and goodness MAKING NEW, each and every day, the work of Creation. How great are your creatures, YHVH, all beings made with Godly wisdom. Blessed are You, RENEWING each day the work of creation.

Gratitude Journal: The easiest way to do this is to purchase a small journal and keep it by your bed. Each night, before you go to sleep, write down three to five things from your day that you are grateful for. Pay attention to "daily miracles": you might write down things you take for granted, like having shelter, or food, or running water. If something difficult happened that day, see if you can find anything in connection to it for which to be grateful— perhaps your own restraint from making the situation worse, or a learning you are taking from it, or an awareness of your own resilience. Jot down small things you might have noticed over the course of the day, whether a stranger's smile on the street or a sweet birdsong. It doesn't matter that much what you write about; the practice is taking the time to express gratitude in a sincere way.

Sending and Receiving Gratitude: There is power in thanking others, and we can take this on as a practice. Whether you send a handwritten note or an email or a message via social media to someone you know, or just make a special effort to say a heartfelt thank-you to a salesperson across the counter, make sure to express your gratitude to someone in your life at least once a day. Be creative! You can expand the practice by setting a higher number of people to thank each day. You can also practice receiving gratitude. It has become commonplace in our culture to brush aside the gratitude expressed by others with responses like "No problem" or "It's nothing." But we diminish the gratitude of others when we don't receive it fully. Try responding with a good old-fashioned "You are very welcome," or "I am so glad you liked it," or "My pleasure." Think of sending and receiving gratitude as a kind of prayer practice, to be taken on with sincerity and an open heart.

Embracing Uncertainty

One of my favorite Jewish blessings is said after eating a simple meal. It begins this way:

> Blessed are you, YHVH, who creates many and various living beings with their *chisronot,* their deficiencies.

What stands out to me about this blessing is the praise of the Creator not just for making the marvelous variety of life but also our "deficiencies," our lacks. We are created lacking, in order that we can be filled up. Instead of feeling anguish over the ways in which we are not complete, the empty spaces that are not yet filled, we can bless them as opportunities, and even rejoice in the imperfection that we share with all of Creation. I take this blessing as a directive to find ways to embrace my uncertainties, the unknowns and unfulfilled places in myself and my life. Here are a few practices to enhance our ability to embrace uncertainty:

Curiosity Practices: In her book *The Wisdom of Not Knowing: Discovering a Life of Wonder by Embracing Uncertainty,* psychotherapist and rabbinic pastor Estelle Frankel suggests a wonderful way to go through a regular day:

> Try and slow down and take note of all the wondrous things in your life that nourish and support you . . . As you observe the familiar people and objects in our life, pause to ask yourself, "What is this?" Notice how this question heightens your awareness.[21]

We unconsciously spend an inordinate amount of time during our day categorizing and having opinions about things. It's all part of a habit of wanting our world to make sense and line up. Asking, "What is this?," disrupts that habit, and helps open up our perception. We can take on the mindset of a toddler, looking with curiosity and occasional amazement at the most mundane of objects. Try it when you go on a walk or talk with someone or eat breakfast. Looking at a bush or a telephone pole or a face or a bowl of cereal, gently ask, "What is this?" See if anything surprising results!

This type of question can also be used in meditation. If you have a regular meditation practice, try asking open-ended questions as you sit and notice your experience. When first taking your seat, you can ask: "How do I know I am sitting?" As a physical sensation or a thought arises, ask: "What is this?" The purpose is not to then go into an extended intellectual discourse about the nature of sitting or thinking. It is to bring real curiosity to your experience.

Another practice that Frankel suggests is keeping a curiosity journal. The idea is to try to come up with one good question each day, a question that opens up your imagination. Some questions she suggests include "Where is this experience taking me?" or "Who might I become if I follow this path?" or "What meaning can I derive from this experience?" Frankel writes: "Good questions open us up to unknown possibilities, to the future, while nonproductive questions tend to be ruminative, rehashing things from the past that cannot be undone."[22] So in a difficult moment, try to avoid "Why is this happening to me?" or

"Why are those people so terrible?" and try instead to dive into the dilemma, looking for a question that might shift your perspective in a new and helpful way. You might combine your gratitude journal with the curiosity journal as a "becoming journal," fostering a sense of both appreciation and wonder as you go about your day.

Teach Your Tongue to Say, "I Don't Know": There is a famous saying in the Talmud, "Teach your tongue to say 'I do not know.'"[23] I thought about this teaching quite a bit during the COVID-19 pandemic, when it became nearly impossible to plan anything more than a few days ahead. I decided that "I don't know" would become my mantra. I made signs with these words on it, and put them up all over my home office. When I would find myself getting anxious as I started thinking about planning the High Holy Days or the congregational calendar for the coming year, I would say to myself, "I don't know." The effects of this simple practice were quite amazing. I went from feeling almost constantly anxious and constricted to feeling open and even happy. Those words—*I don't know*—were like a get-out-of-jail free card, releasing me from the responsibility of being certain about anything.

The Talmud quote has a second half: "Teach your tongue to say 'I don't know,' lest you make things up and become trapped." That is, sometimes we say stuff just to act like we know, and then we become trapped in the false reality that our words have created. It is far more honest—and far more liberating—to simply say, "I don't know." And the truth is, we really don't. Even in non-pandemic times, anything can happen. We can fight that reality or embrace it. In my experience, I suffer a lot less when I can simply admit, "I don't know."

There are many ways to practice "I don't know." One is putting these words up in as many places as you'd like in your home or office or car, just as reminders (if you know Hebrew, the phrase is "*Aini yodea*"). It can also be a helpful phrase to bring to mind when you find your mind racing with planning or when anxiety arises at the thought of something you need to do. Simply say to yourself, "I don't know." When facing an uncertain situation, put some music on and dance around, singing as loud as you can, "I DON'T KNOW!"

Ehyeh *Is with You*

In addition to embracing the truth of "I don't know," we can also cultivate a sense of God's presence in our moments of instability and uncertainty. An awareness of the Power of Becoming working through us and within us can hold us up as we step off the cliff into the unknown.

Walking Meditation: Find a space in which you can walk about seven or eight paces. Set an intention to be aware of each step, and then walk slowly and mindfully, paying attention to the sensations in your feet or in your legs as you go. When you get to the end of your short path, pay close attention as you turn. The moments of turning, of transition, tend to be the moments of instability. As you turn, you can say, "*Ehyeh* is with me." Walk mindfully back in the other direction, and again, as you turn, say, "*Ehyeh* is with me," or "*Ehyeh imach,*" the words that YHVH said to Moses at the bush. Do this walking meditation for ten or more minutes, paying attention to your steps, and to the moments of turning. See what you notice as you walk. Invite the Power of Becoming into each step.

10

. . . . .

THE MATERIAL WORLD

We are living in the material world, and I am a material girl.
—*Peter Brown and Robert Rans, "Material Girl"*

A fundamental teaching of Jewish mysticism is that the created world is God's "garment," a physical cloak that hides the divine Presence of which we are a part. The spiritual task is to perceive the godliness hidden within the material world, and to become aware that all of the distinctions we perceive between people, between different life-forms, are surface appearance and essentially unreal. Ultimately, there is only God. This is how the mystics understand the biblical claim that God is "One": the divine is the Oneness in which we are located, and with proper training and intent it is possible for the spiritual seeker to experience this Oneness. If we only had the ability to see it, we would realize that we are not separate from one another or from God.

While I do not doubt those who have experienced a sense of merger with the divine Oneness, and while I deeply appreciate the profound lesson of connectedness that emerges from this teaching, I would suggest that the mystical understanding of God as "One" is another metaphor. It is a beautiful, powerful way to affirm both an experience of connection with the world around us, and the essential godliness of Creation. Where I diverge from the classical mystical understanding is my conviction that the "garment" of material reality doesn't hide God's essence—quite the opposite. The realm of divinity, of the spirit, is not more real or more valuable than the realm of the physical. In fact, it is only by taking very seriously our physical experience of this material world that we can access the divine Presence at all. We are embodied creatures, and through a multitude of metaphors based in our bodily experiences, our brains and our hearts can access profound spiritual awareness.

Each of the metaphors I have explored in this book are rooted in my ancestors' lived experience of the physical world. Many of these metaphors—Rock, Fire, Water, Voice—are found in numerous religious traditions, as they are fundamental aspects of life on this planet. But we need not only to look to ancient texts for accessible metaphors for the divine. In this chapter, I'd like to explore a couple of modern metaphors from the realms of science and technology.

Electricity

A few years into my rabbinate, I was on a retreat with about thirty other rabbis from across the Jewish denominations. On the opening night, we did a get-to-know-you exercise in which we had a series of three-minute conversations with one another, each with a different prompt. As I moved around the circle of colleagues, I prepared to answer the question, "If you hadn't become a rabbi, and money or ability or prerequisite knowledge were not an issue, what would you have been?" I was pretty sure I was going to say I'd have been a community organizer. I had worked in a variety of progressive organizations before going to rabbinical school, and I identified as a social justice activist. So imagine my surprise when it was my turn to answer the question and what came out of my mouth was: "I would have been a physicist."

The reason I found this completely surprising is that I am terrible at math and never got anywhere near a physics class in my high school or college years. There is no one less likely to have become a physicist than I. But after I gave my answer, I realized that I do share something with those who are blessed to do physics: a sense of wonder at the universe, and a deep desire to understand how things work. As a rabbi, I get to engage in big questions, and I seek to discern some kind of meaningful order in what often feels like a disordered, chaotic world. I want to know what makes us tick, and what the larger context is for human existence. And while I can't really fathom what physicists do, I wonder if some of the same desires and curiosities are at play.

When I read the Hebrew Bible, I imagine that its authors were sort of like me, and sort of like modern physicists, seeking answers to how the cosmos works and what our place in it is. Their experience of the divine was part of that exploration—was, in fact, inseparable from it. Science offers metaphors that help me understand some of the more challenging aspects of the biblical portrayal of God.

Among the most difficult stories in the Bible are those in which seemingly unsuspecting characters get "zapped" by God. A good example is the story of Nadav and Avihu that I described in chapter 8. Aaron's oldest sons make an unauthorized offering at the altar, and are immediately consumed by the divine Fire. Something similar happens in the Book of Samuel, when King David attempts to bring the ark of the covenant—a golden box holding the stone tablets that Moses received on Mount Sinai—to his capital city of Jerusalem. The ark is being transported on an ox-cart, and when the oxen stumble, one of the men guiding the cart—a guy named Uzzah—reaches out to steady the ark. When he touches it, YHVH is "incensed" and strikes him down, and Uzzah dies.[1]

This story seems even worse than the episode with Na-dav and Avihu. They at least could be accused of making a dubious offering in an irresponsible way. All that poor Uzzah did was try to keep the holy ark from falling out of a cart. Why in the world would God strike him down?

Earlier in the Bible, the Israelites are warned that only the tribe of the Levites are authorized to transport the various items of the Mishkan, the holy tabernacle. And the men responsible for transporting the ark—via a set of poles fastened to rings on its sides—have to be extremely careful not to actually touch it, or they will die. When God "strikes" Uzzah in the story of the oxcart, it seems to be the unavoidable consequence of someone touching a holy object that is profoundly dangerous to humans.

The best that I can understand how the ancient Israelites understood this holy danger is through the metaphor of electricity. The Holy of Holies at the center of the Mishkan housed the ark, which functioned something like the core of a nuclear reactor, supplying the sacred energy that was then channeled by the priests through their rituals. Just as enormous precautions have to be taken to safely make use of nuclear energy, so too did those who interacted with the Mishkan and the ark at its center have to take extreme care not to get zapped.

When the Book of Samuel describes God being "incensed" when Uzzah touches the ark, we can understand it less as the emotion of anger and more like a natural physical reaction. It's akin to me being able to safely use the electric power that is supplied to my home as long as it is wired and grounded properly. I need to avoid sticking my finger in a socket. Hapless Uzzah had the best of intentions, but by touching the ark, he did the biblical equivalent of holding up a metal rod in a lightning storm, and got a shock that took his life.

The question remains, why did the authors of the Bible perceive godly power as so inherently dangerous? What truth were they trying to convey in these metaphors of fire and electricity and the stories of "zapping" that happens to people both innocent and guilty?

My answer is that the biblical authors were acknowledging a simple reality: to be alive is pretty damn scary.

We exist in a universe that is largely, even today, beyond our understanding. We are often at the mercy of forces we cannot control. The ancients were very honest about God, and the Bible is not a Hallmark greeting card. It is a holy, sometimes contradictory muddle of beauty and horror, love and pain, hope and hopelessness. A lot like life. And somewhere within and behind all of this complexity is YHVH, the Source of Life Itself.

As the prophet Isaiah audaciously declared: *"Forming light and creating darkness, making peace and creating destruction—I YHVH do all these things."* There is only one Power Source of the universe, the prophet teaches. It manifests in that which we find pleasant and in that which scares us. It both sustains us and makes us mortal. And just as with electrical current, if we don't properly channel that divine Power, we can generate some severe shocks. As the world witnessed in Hiroshima and Nagasaki in 1945, when human beings start playing with the primal energies of the universe, we take on Godlike powers of both creation and destruction. Perhaps the Bible was right in warning us that there are some things that we humans should just not touch.

Plugging In

When I was poking around on the internet with the question "What is electricity?" (because, as I said, I never studied this!), I found this intriguing answer:

Electricity is all around us—powering technology like our cell phones, computers, lights, soldering irons, and air conditioners. It's tough to escape it in our modern world. Even when you try to escape electricity, it's still at work throughout nature, from the lightning in a thunderstorm to the synapses inside our body. But what exactly is electricity? This is a very complicated question, and as you dig deeper and ask more questions, there really is not a definitive answer, only abstract representations of how electricity interacts with our surroundings.[2]

I love this reticence to give a "definitive answer" to my question, an acknowledgment that in the realm of science as well as in the realm of religion, there remain some questions that resist the limits of human explanation. One could easily change the question to "What is God?" and rework the answer to say: "This is a very complicated question, and as you dig deeper and ask more questions, there really is not a definitive answer, only abstract representations of how God interacts with our surroundings."

But we do know some things about electricity. At its root, it is the movement of electrons, and electrons are among the fundamental building blocks of the universe. To think about the divine as Electricity is to affirm the godly energy that moves within us and within all of Creation. God as Electricity also invites us to think about how we can connect in productive and energizing ways to the kinetic Divine Flow.

There is a famous Talmudic teaching that a person should say one hundred blessings a day.[3] Not wanting to leave this to chance, the early rabbis came up with many ways to fulfill this requirement, from reciting the blessings contained in the daily liturgy to saying a blessing over every kind of food that goes into our mouths. There are blessings for waking up, washing, putting on clothes, going to the bathroom, seeing a rainbow, doing something for the first time, studying, celebrating Shabbat and holidays, and many more. It is a kind of Jewish mindfulness practice, in which I need to stop, notice what I am doing, remember which blessing goes with which action, and then recite the blessing.

The rabbis also standardized the form of the blessings we say. Each one begins, "Blessed are you, YHVH our

God, Sovereign Power of the Universe, That . . ." The remainder of the blessing names a godly action associated with whatever it is we're about to do. When I eat a carrot, I bless That which "creates the fruit of the earth." When I put on my clothes in the morning, I bless That which "clothes the naked." When I poop, I bless That which "created the human with wisdom, and made within us openings and channels" (this is one of my favorite blessings!). The people who wrote these blessings knew that God did not literally make the food we eat or the clothes we wear. Rather, saying a blessing makes a connection between my physical existence and the sacred processes that enable me to live and thrive.

If God is Electricity, then saying a blessing is a way of "plugging in" to the current. The carrot on my plate represents the combined energy of earth, sun, and rain; farmer and farm equipment; transportation and markets. When I say my blessing, I acknowledge the divinity that runs through it all. There is another Talmudic teaching that if we enjoy something of this world without saying a blessing, it is akin to stealing. I take this to mean that when we say a blessing before making use of something, we are giving credit where credit is due—to all those elements and creatures involved along the way, all the way back to the divine Power Source Itself. To ignore the blessing is to "steal" that credit, to pretend that we did it all ourselves, and to erase the connection we share both with our divine Source and those who make our sustenance and well-being possible.

Godly Positioning System

Many years ago I heard a story about a man in Germany with an early GPS system in his car. He was driving along and started noticing people outside waving their arms and shouting at him. He ignored them and kept driving, and then ignored some flashing red lights, and the next thing he knew, he had driven into a river. Apparently, the car's GPS thought that there was a bridge where, in fact, there was only a ferry.

Luckily, the man was fine, but the episode revealed the extent to which we will ignore the very obvious signs the world gives us. I experienced my own version of this when Gina and I spent a month in Seville, Spain. We rented a car for an overnight excursion to Grenada, and on the way back, we decided to visit the small town where the poet Federico García Lorca was born. Using the GPS in the rental car, we found the Lorca museum and enjoyed our visit there. When it was time to head back out to the highway, the GPS gave us directions that took us to a different road from the one we had come in on. It was pretty obvious, in this small town, that there was only one road to and from the main highway. But despite my misgivings, I listened to the authoritative British female voice issuing from the dashboard, following its instructions until we ended up at the end of a gravel road in a field.

Why did I—why did the German man—continue to follow instructions that were so obviously wrong? Why did we ignore the evidence of our eyes and ears and our own common sense? I don't really know the answer, but the question makes me wonder about who and what we give authority to in our lives. Which directions do I follow, and which do I ignore? Why are some voices compelling, even when I know they are probably leading me in the wrong direction? How do I navigate my way through life, and how have I learned which voices—both internal and external—to trust?

As I reflect on all the different pathways I have gone down over the years, the choices I have made and the questions I continue to face, I am aware of something I might call a divine GPS—a Godly Positioning System—that has helped guide me along the way. It's a subtle sort of guide; at no point have I had an experience of a disembodied voice insistently telling me which way to turn. But there have been moments of listening and discerning, of taking a step in a new direction, of following what my heart and mind tell me is the right thing to do, that have led me to who I am today. I have relied on Something beyond my own limited awareness in those moments to take the steps I have needed to take, and been able to trust that the choices I have made were wholesome ones. And so far, I have not yet been guided into the spiritual equivalent of a river or an empty field.

Where Are You?

The GPS apps on our phones and in our cars rely on multiple components:

- satellite signals which determine our location;
- mapping software that tells us which roads go from here to there; and
- traffic data that influences which routes a GPS app will suggest.

Taken together, this technology does a remarkable job of finding ways to get from point A to point B, even with the occasional glitches and misdirections.

GPS is made possible by over thirty satellites orbiting Earth, constantly sending out signals that are read by our devices down here on the ground. Once the receiver in the device has calculated its distance from at least four satellites, it can accurately locate itself (and the person holding it). Similarly, if a Godly Positioning System is to be effective in our lives, we need to begin by figuring out where we are.

Interestingly, the very first question in the Torah is one of positioning. Right after they have eaten the forbidden fruit of the Tree of Knowledge of Good and Evil, God asks Adam and Eve: "*Ayeka*—Where are you?"[4] As I mentioned in chapter 5, this isn't really a question about physical place. The "where" of God's question has more to do with spiritual and ethical location. "Why are you hiding from Me?" God may have been asking. Or perhaps, "Where do you humans now fit in the scheme of Creation, having taken on this new ability to choose between good and evil?"

This positioning vis-à-vis the divine comes up in significant moments in the life journeys of other biblical characters. Abraham, Moses, and the prophets Samuel and Isaiah answer God's call by saying, "*Hineni*"—"Here I am." Again, this is not a matter of physical location but a statement about emotional and spiritual presence. I am ready, the characters are saying, for what will be asked of me. I am ready to become who I need to be. "Where are you?" is really a question of "*Who* are you?"

My own life journey has been an ongoing process of figuring out who I am and where I am located. In my younger years, a lot of this figuring out had to do with the messages I received about who I was, or should be, based on my physical body. I am female, and use the pronoun "she," but by first grade, I knew I was lousy at being a girl. For example, kids in my elementary school played a game that for the life of me I couldn't see the point of, in which the boys would chase the girls on the playground. In a not unfriendly way, the boys learned pretty soon to say, "Let's chase the girls—except Toba!" I had somehow communicated my disinterest in this particular gendered activity. By second grade, I had stopped wearing skirts and dresses, and I spent the rest of my young years being called a boy by those who did not know me, both because of how I dressed and because my mother dealt with my unruly curly hair by cutting it very short. I knew I wasn't a boy, and I felt embarrassed when people thought I was one, but I was also clear that I preferred GI Joes to dolls and wouldn't have been caught dead learning ballet or joining the Girl Scouts.

In retrospect, I now see that I had somehow located myself outside of the gender binary that defined the world around me. At the time it wasn't easy, and included some unpleasant moments of being told I was in the wrong dressing room. But I now appreciate how this experience of having to claim a space that was particularly "Toba," outside of others' assumptions and definitions, was a very important one in my spiritual development. I intuitively learned that what the world tells us about ourselves is not necessarily true. I also learned that some of the systems by which people organize themselves are pretty ridiculous, which has fed a healthy desire to inquire into better possible systems of organization.

One of our most basic spiritual tasks is to foster an awareness of who we really are, a sense of our "location" vis-à-vis everyone around us. It's a process of saying *Hineni*—I am *here*—both to ourselves and to others. *This* is me. It can be challenging to locate ourselves outside of the assumptions, expectations, and negative messages that the world hands us. The Godly Positioning System is That which teaches us to trust our own sense of ourselves. We can experience this divine GPS internally, in our innate sense of who we are. We can also experience it externally, in the wholesome messages we receive from the people around us, the loving voices that affirm our humanity and our unique gifts. And of course, our location is not static. As we discover new facets of who we are and who we want to be, we can continue to ask ourselves that godly question: "Where am I?"

In the months leading up to the 2020 elections, when there was so much negativity and hatred in the air, I discovered the streaming show *Queer Eye*. In this reboot of the original *Queer Eye for the Straight Guy*, five gay men spend a week with someone nominated by friends and family for a life makeover. No longer just for "the straight guy," the Fab Five visit a wide range of people in need of some confidence-boosting and self-care, people of all ages and ethnic backgrounds and walks of life. On the surface level, the *Queer Eye* cast help with personal grooming and home design and cooking and wardrobe, plus emotional help dealing with whatever internal obstacles might be keeping that week's hero from being open to change. The deeper intent of the makeover is to boost each person's self-confidence and ability to feel at home in themselves and their surroundings. It is a process of affirming each person's ability to fully say *Hineni*, "Here I am!" in every aspect of their lives.

I soon found myself watching the show as a kind of spiritual practice. As the world appeared to be crumbling around me, every episode reaffirmed my faith in humanity. The Fab Five are experts at helping each person they work with see their own unique beauty and gifts. This often involves some measure of healing from negative messages they've internalized because of their race or sexuality or life experiences. Antoni, Tan, Bobby, Karamo, and Jonathan are a Godly Positioning System love-bomb, helping their "heroes" get back on track with humor and care, plus a nice haircut and new furniture.

The Map and the Minyan

I have dedicated much of my adult life to teaching about Judaism and building a community dedicated to Jewish practice. I do this because of the deep wisdom I find in Jewish texts and traditions. Judaism, like other wisdom traditions, functions like mapping software. Prayer, study, meditation, observing the Sabbath, caring for the sick, refraining from harmful speech, giving away a portion of our income—all these traditional practices are pathways to spiritual awareness and ethical living. And as with mapping software, there are multiple ways to get from here to there. Some people may be more drawn to intense prayer or meditation practice, others to study of sacred text, others to taking religious teachings into the streets. The spiritual task is to learn to read the data in the map, in order to be able to follow its instructions and choose the best path.

One of the dangers in mapping software is that parts of the data can become outdated. Judaism certainly has its share of painful teachings that reflect a world of the distant past, with assumptions about women, about queer people, about those who are not Jewish, about people with disabilities, and more, that range from ignorant to actively harmful. I think of these as old roads that go nowhere, and must now be either entirely removed from our mapping data, or changed enough so that we can get where we need to go without running ourselves or anyone else off the road.

Learning to read the map is where practice and discipline come in. Our "grab and go" culture would have us believe that spiritual attainments can be found easily and quickly. And while I enjoy watching *Queer Eye,* I know that no one's life is actually transformed in a week. The Godly Positioning System requires commitment to learning and incorporating the mapping data, whether that's a regular yoga practice or daily meditation, observing Shabbat or conscientiously fostering qualities of patience, gratitude, and joy.

The final component of the Godly Positioning System is the data we receive from other travelers. This is the real-time information about crashes and backups, potholes and roadwork. Here, the divine is manifest in community, in all those traveling along with us. On the journey, we each contribute information and receive it. As I learn from my mistakes, I can share my learning. As I observe others stumble, I can take note and try to avoid that particular obstacle.

Learning with and from others is essential to making our journey successful.

Every spiritual tradition has its version of sacred, supportive community: for Christians, the church; for Buddhists, the sangha; for Jews, the *minyan*—a quorum of ten adults needed for communal prayer. Community holds us accountable, and also gives us support. You might think that it doesn't matter whether you are alone or in a group when you're sitting in silent meditation, but my experience is that it's a whole lot harder to just give up and get off the cushion when you're surrounded by other people (even on Zoom!). In the Jewish practice of Mussar, the cultivation of wholesome qualities of heart and mind, it is traditional to work with a *va'ad*, a small group of fellow students who help keep one another on track through regular meetings. Alcoholics Anonymous is perhaps one of the best examples of the power of this aspect of GPS, bringing together people on a journey of healing who benefit profoundly from the honest sharing of both mistakes and successes.

I am drawn to the metaphor of the Godly Positioning System because we are living in such profoundly destabilizing, disorienting times. It can be really hard to know what to do, day by day, minute by minute. I think we all long for some steady voice, issuing out of our minds' dashboards, telling us exactly when and where to turn. And while I don't think such an authoritative voice exists, I do believe we can learn to trust the divine GPS. We always have available to us these things: our ability to locate ourselves; spiritual teachings both ancient and new to guide us; and community to accompany us on the journey.

God as Electricity and GPS Practices

Plugging In: A practice of saying daily blessings is a powerful way to "plug in" to the Divine Power Source. A blessing is an acknowledgment that our lives are dependent on the earth and on other people, and that through it all runs a sacred Current of Life. It is also a way of remembering the connections we share that are often invisible. As Dr. Martin Luther King Jr. famously wrote:

It really all boils down to this: that all life is interrelated . . . Did you ever stop to think that you can't leave for your job in the morning without being dependent on most of the world? You get up in the morning and go to the bathroom and reach over for the sponge, and that's handed to you by a Pacific Islander. You reach for a bar of soap, and that's given to you at the hands of a Frenchman. And then you go into the kitchen to drink your coffee, and that's poured into your cup by a South American . . . And then you reach for your toast, and that's given to you at the hands of an English-speaking farmer, not to mention the baker. And before you finish eating breakfast in the morning, you've depended on more than half the world.[5]

To acknowledge all that goes into bringing us the food on which we depend, Judaism has developed a system of food blessings. A different blessing is said depending on what I am about to eat, which means I have to pause for a moment before putting something in my mouth. I highly recommend this practice, whether you say the blessings every time you eat, or choose one meal a day to remind yourself. Here are the traditional blessings in Hebrew, along with my translations into English:

Before eating a meal that includes bread (including tortillas, pizza dough, sandwich bread, etc.):

Baruch atah Adonai, Eloheinu melech ha-olam, hamotzi lechem min ha-aretz.
Blessed are you, YHVH, Power Source, bringing forth bread from the earth.

Before eating cereal, cakes, cookies, or grains not made into bread:

Baruch atah Adonai, Eloheinu melech ha-olam, borei minei m'zonot.
Blessed are you, YHVH, Power Source, creating all kinds of foods.

Before eating fruit that grows on trees and vines (nuts, tree fruits, avocados, grapes, etc.):

Baruch atah Adonai, Eloheinu melech ha-olam, borei p'ri ha-etz.
Blessed are you, YHVH, Power Source, creating fruit of the tree.

Before eating vegetables and fruit that grow in the ground (strawberries, zucchini, tomatoes, potatoes, etc.):

Baruch atah Adonai, Eloheinu melech ha-olam, borei p'ri ha-adama.
Blessed are you, YHVH, Power Source, creating fruit of the earth.

Before eating anything else (including all animal products):

Baruch atah Adonai, Eloheinu melech ha-olam, sh'hakol nihiyeh bid'varo.
Blessed are you, YHVH, Power Source, Creator of all.

If memorizing all of these different blessings feels like too much, then I invite you to come up with your own blessing practice. The important elements are the pause before putting something in your mouth, the reflection on what it is that you are about to eat, and the acknowledgment that there is a Current of Life that has provided you with nourishment.

Hineni / Here I Am: Judaism teaches that every human being has, at their core, a *neshama tehora,* a pure soul. The Talmud says that when we wake up in the morning, the first thing we should say is, "My God, the soul you have given me is pure," to remind ourselves of this basic fact. It can be very stabilizing to connect to the essential, unique core of my humanity, my *neshama tehora,* the pure soul within me. It is a way to remember my "location," my relationship both to the holiness within me and around me. Whatever is happening around us, we each have the ability to say *Hineni,* "I am here," this is who I am. This body, this heart, this spirit, right here.

To follow the Talmud's advice, take a few minutes each morning to meditate using these words:

Elohai neshama sh'natatah bee tehora hee.
My God, the soul you have given me is pure.

The word *neshama* means "soul," but it is very closely related to the word for breath, *nishimah.* These words are a wonderful opportunity for a breath-focused meditation. Even if you don't speak Hebrew, using the Hebrew words as a kind of mantra can be helpful, because each word ends with a vowel, an opportunity to release the out-breath. Here is how the words sound (the capitalized syllable of each word is emphasized):

- el-oh-HI
- neh-shah-MAH
- sheh-nah-TAH-tah
- BEE
- Teh-hore-AH
- HEE

Take a breath in, gently say the beginning of each word, and then say the last syllable on the out-breath. You can do this out loud, or silently if you prefer, one word per breath.

As you do the meditation, invite some appreciation of who you are in this moment. Reflect on your positive attributes, or a recent action you've taken that's beneficial. Use this meditation as an opportunity to "locate" yourself as you start your day. You might also set an intention for your day—to respond with kindness to whatever arises, or to bring a bit of joy to those around you, or to be gentle with yourself.

If difficult thoughts or feelings arise as you attempt this meditation, pay attention. This might be a course-correction indicator. What feels amiss? If you find that it is difficult to feel good about yourself, if you are feeling lost or off course, then it might be time to check in with the Godly Positioning System. You can ask the question "Where am I?" and then just sit quietly, and see what arises in response. You might not get a useful answer right away, and that's okay. Just becoming aware that you've gotten off track can be helpful. Think about who, or what, functions for you like the GPS satellites, sending signals that help you locate yourself. Have some conversations with those people, or engage in the activities that nourish your spirit. Have faith that, with some help, you can locate yourself once again.

Bechira Points: Rabbi Eliyahu Dessler, a twentieth-century teacher of Jewish ethics, laid out a path of spiritual growth that resembles an ongoing navigational challenge. Rabbi Dessler taught that at many moments in our lives, we encounter what he called *bechira*—choice—points. These are moments in which our negative habits or inclinations bump up against our positive inclinations, and we feel like we are facing a choice. For example, I am in general an honest person, and would not steal something from a store. Walking up and down the aisles, I do not experience any desire to pull something off the shelf and hide it in my pocket. But if I'm at the checkout and the cashier fails to ring up one of my items, I experience it as a *bechira* point: Do I tell the cashier, or not? On my good days, I will decide yes, and let them know. But on days when I am feeling rushed or grumpy or that the world owes me something, I might not. In this moment, I experience a struggle between my deeper values, what I know to be true, and a kind of dishonesty in which I make excuses for behavior I know is not right.

Rabbi Dessler teaches that when I choose to do the correct, honest thing, I experience spiritual growth. The more times I make that decision, the less I experience it as a choice, until I am habituated to always do the right thing in that situation.

In the metaphor of God as GPS, we can imagine ourselves checking our Godly Positioning System each time we encounter a *bechira* point. Which way should I turn? What is the ethical, the helpful, the healthy thing to do? Much of the time, we act out of habit. We open the refrigerator door whether or not we are hungry; we compulsively check our email; we avoid situations that might require us to sacrifice our comfort; we stay silent when we should speak up or speak harshly when we should be quiet. Yet each time that we encounter a *bechira* point, the Godly Positioning System is giving us an opportunity to choose the path of awareness. When we make choices that align with our values, when we are able to not succumb to negative habits or irrational fears, we strengthen our capacity for true freedom.

It is helpful to become aware of *bechira* points when they arise, as they become a kind of personal curriculum for moral and spiritual growth. If, for example, I get habitually angry in certain situations and lash out at others, I don't experience any choice; I am simply reacting. But if I can become more mindful of my own emotions, and am able to hit Pause on my reactions, then I have created a *bechira* point. Do I need to voice my anger in this moment, or not? If I am trying to get a message across, how might I express myself in an effective way? I may or may not end up making the wisest choice, but in that moment, I have consulted my GPS and am making the effort to take the best action I can.

Building on Rabbi Dessler's teaching about *bechira* points, my colleague Rabbi David Jaffe teaches that we can practice becoming aware of our choice points. He writes: "You know you are in a choice point when you need to struggle to decide what to do . . . With awareness we can assess why we are being pulled in different directions and which side of the choice better reflects reality and truth as we know it."[6] He goes on to suggest that we set aside a time to review the day that just passed, and to identify any choices that caused us struggle or deliberation. Once we have noticed the *bechira* point, we can reflect on what seemed to be pulling us in opposite directions in that moment. What were we choosing between? What values or habits were at play? And finally, regardless of which choice we made, which direction seems to better reflect our deeper values, and which is some form of self-deception?

Try making this a regular practice for a week or two, and see if you notice any patterns in your choice points. Rabbi Jaffe suggests that "choice points will reveal your growing edge, because it is through difficult choices that we emerge from self-deception into greater awareness of reality." And remember that the Godly Positioning System is accompanying you in this practice, and encouraging you to take the path that will ultimately get you where you want to go.

THE END AND THE
BEGINNING

I once heard a mindfulness teacher say, "This practice is simple, but that doesn't mean it's easy." The same could be said about this exploration of God metaphors. The basic premise is fairly simple. As human beings, we are innately attuned to experiences of the sacred, and the only way we can think and talk about those experiences is through metaphors. Because experiences of divinity encompass all aspects of our lives—joy and sorrow, birth and death, love and anger and compassion—and because each of us has our own unique sensibilities, we need a multitude of metaphors to access those experiences. No one metaphor will do. As an ancient midrash teaches, just because we call God different things in different situations doesn't mean there is more than one God. All spiritual traditions recognize this truth, and offer a plethora of metaphors to help us access the divine.

The "not easy" part, at least for those of us raised in the

West, is that we are deeply stuck in the "God is a Big Person" metaphor. When I have taught this material, there has inevitably been one person who insists: "These metaphors are fine, but is it really God?" What they are really saying is: "God is a Being who judges/loves/punishes/forgives, and if Water or Voice or Cloud doesn't do that, it can't really be God." Or sometimes people forget that a metaphor is not a definition. Because "God is a Big Person" is so embedded in our brains, we actually think it is a definition, and so it feels "realer" than a less familiar metaphor like Rock or Electricity.

The "God is a Big Person" metaphor is one that we "live by," whatever we profess to believe or not believe. To come to "live by" other metaphors, we need to make them part of our spiritual practice, part of our conversation, part of our communal worship. Now that you've finished this book, I invite you to start again! Choose one metaphor, one chapter, and spend a few weeks or even months with it. Talk about it with friends. Choose a practice or two, and do them regularly for an extended period of time. Explore! In my experience, the metaphors "work" when we open ourselves to trying on new habits of thought and action.

If any of the metaphors don't speak to you, you have two choices: leave it for now, and stay open to checking it out some other time. Or take up the challenge and try out the practices for that chapter, use those God names, as a way of opening up your mind and heart. Your resistance might be a sign that there is something potentially fruitful to explore. You may be drawn to one metaphor because it fits some preconceived notions you have of what it means to be "spiritual," and a diametrically opposed metaphor will give you access to new ways of experiencing the divine. The main thing to remember is that metaphors aren't "right" or "wrong." They are simply different pathways to the truth of our own experience and of the world around us.

There is a beautiful story in the Mishnah, the earliest collection of rabbinic teachings, about Rabbi Nehunia ben Hakaneh, who would offer a short prayer when he entered and when he left the house of study. When asked what these prayers were, he answered, "When I enter I pray that no mishap should occur through me, and when I leave I express thanks for my portion."[1] In the tradition of Rabbi Nehunia, I pray that the words I have offered here have led no one astray, and I give thanks for this amazing opportunity to share my explorations with you.

ACKNOWLEDGMENTS

. . . .

In many ways I feel less the author of this book and more a vessel for certain teachings to emerge. I owe much to many teachers and colleagues whose wisdom echoes throughout these pages. I have done my best to provide sources for insights that did not originate with me, and apologize for any credit that is owed that I failed to give. I would also like to especially acknowledge those whose teachings helped shape this book: Rabbi Arthur Waskow, my earliest (and ongoing) teacher of Torah; Rabbi Arthur Green, for his teaching and writing; my other teachers at the Reconstructionist Rabbinical College, especially Dr. Tikva Frymer-Kensky (may her memory be for a blessing) and Rabbi Nancy Fuchs Kreimer; my colleagues and teachers Rabbis Shefa Gold, David Jaffe, and Sheila Peltz Weinberg; Rabbi Goldie Milgram, for sharing her work on metaphors for the divine; theologian Sally McFague, for her groundbreaking work on God and metaphor; and my teachers of mindfulness meditation, especially Sylvia Boorstein, Christina Feldman, and Narayan Helen Liebenson.

ACKNOWLEDGMENTS

I owe profound gratitude to the feminist and womanist writers and theologians whose work has inspired me and paved the way for this book, including Mary Daly, Alice Walker, Judith Plaskow, Rebecca Alpert, Carter Heyward, Katie Cannon, and Marcia Falk. I also owe profound gratitude to my congregants at Congregation Dorshei Tzedek, who were my first students in this exploration of God in metaphor; thank you for taking this journey with me. Thank you to Craig Levine, for making the connection that brought me to St Martin's Press, and to Michael Flamini and Amy Hughes for encouragement and patience with this first-time author. Deep gratitude to Julie Leavitt, for support, wisdom, and encouraging me to explore these metaphors in my own life. And last but far from least, love and gratitude to my family and friends for all the cheerleading along the way.

While parts of this book were written in a variety of locations, the majority of my time writing and editing was done on land within the territory of the Massachusett, Pawtucket, and their neighbors—the Wampanoag and Nipmuc Peoples. I owe profound gratitude to these nations for their stewardship of this land over hundreds of generations. May this book be one step toward healing and justice for all who dwell on this earth.

NOTES
• • • • • •

1. Metaphorically Speaking

1. James Geary, *I Is an Other: The Secret Life of Metaphor and How It Shapes the Way We See the World* (New York: Harper Perennial, 2011), p. 88.

2. George Lakoff and Mark Johnson, *Metaphors We Live By* (Chicago: University of Chicago Press, 1980), chapter 10.

3. Ibid., p. 158.

4. Theodore L. Brown, *Making Truth: Metaphor in Science* (Champaign: University of Illinois Press, 2003), p. 51.

2. The God Metaphor

1. Mary Oliver, "Poem (The Spirit Likes to Dress Up)," in *Dream Work* (New York: Atlantic Monthly Press, 1986).

2. James Geary, *I Is an Other: The Secret Life of Metaphor and How It Shapes the Way We See the World* (New York: Harper Perennial, 2011), p. 25.

3. Barbara J. King, *Evolving God: A Provocative View on the Origins of Religion* (New York: Doubleday, 2008), chapter 5.

4. Ibid., p. 2.

5. Ibid., p. 178.

6. Rabbi David E. S. Stein explores the use of human as well as non-human metaphors in ancient Near Eastern religions and the Hebrew Bible in "On Beyond Gender: Representation of God in the Torah and in Three Recent Renditions into English," *Nashim: A Journal of Jewish Women's Studies & Gender Issues* 15 (Spring 2008).

7. Indeed, even the distinctive Israelite name for God—represented by four Hebrew letters, Yud-Hay-Vav-Hay—seems to have been difficult if not impossible to actually say. This may have been another way to avoid limiting our conception of the divine.

8. James L. Kugel, *The God of Old: Inside the Lost World of the Bible* (New York: Free Press, 2003), pp. 35–36.

9. Ibid., p. 64.

10. Ibid., p. 193, emphasis added.
11. George Lakoff and Mark Johnson, *Metaphors We Live By* (Chicago: University of Chicago Press, 1980), p. 158.
12. The English name Jehovah is an attempt to vocalize these letters, as is Yahweh, but neither is used in Jewish tradition, and in general we refrain from even attempting to pronounce this name.

3. Drinking from God

1. Genesis 1:1–2. This translation, a very literal rendering of the Hebrew, is from Everett Fox, *The Five Books of Moses* (New York: Schocken Books, 2000).
2. Leviticus 8:6. Unless otherwise noted, all English translations of Biblical texts are the author's.
3. Deuteronomy 8:7.
4. Psalms 36:8–11, Psalms 63:2, Psalms 42:2.
5. Isaiah 58:11.
6. Isaiah 12:2–3.
7. Jeremiah 2:13.
8. See Psalms 36:9 and 65:10.
9. Claire Sissons, "What Is the Average Percentage of Water in the Human Body?," *Medical News Today,* May 27, 2020, https://www.medicalnewstoday.com/articles/what-percentage-of-the-human-body-is-water#where-in-the-body.
10. Isaiah 43:2, English translation by Rabbi Shefa Gold. You can hear the chant here - https://www.rabbishefagold.com/through-the-waters/.
11. Deuteronomy 11:13–17.
12. Klaus Koch, *The Prophets: The Assyrian Period* (Philadelphia: Fortress Press, 1983), pp. 58–59.
13. Isaiah 1:21–30.
14. Isaiah 58:11.
15. Amos 5:24.
16. Hosea 10:12.
17. Hosea 10:12.
18. Shefa Gold, *The Magic of Hebrew Chant* (Woodstock, VT: Jewish Lights Publishing, 2013), p. 41.

19. Shema Shlomo, quoted in Yitzhak Buxbaum, *Jewish Spiritual Practices* (Oxford, UK: Jason Aronson, 1990), p. 77.

4. How Awesome Is This Place

1. Mishnah Brachot 5:1.
2. Babylonian Talmud, Shabbat 12b.
3. Genesis 28:17.
4. R. Aharon II of Karlin, in *Itturei Torah,* (Tel Aviv: Yavneh Publishing House, 1996) on Genesis 28:17.
5. With thanks to Cantor Jessi Roemer for pointing out this connection to me.
6. Exodus 33:18, 21.
7. Exodus 34:6–7.

5. If You Truly Listen

1. Exodus 19:16–18.
2. Exodus 19:19, 20:1.
3. Deuteronomy 5:19–25.
4. I am indebted to Val Webb's book *Like Catching Water in a Net: Human Attempts to Describe the Divine* (New York: Continuum, 2007), for insights into the metaphor of God as "communication"—see chapter 6, "Feathers on the Breath of God."
5. Genesis 3:8.
6. Genesis 3:9.
7. Genesis 4:9.
8. Genesis 4:10.
9. Julian Treasure, *How to Be Heard: Secrets for Powerful Speaking and Listening* (Coral Gables, FL: Mango Media, 2017).
10. Evelyn Glennie, "Hearing Essay," January 1, 2015, https://www.evelyn.co.uk/hearing-essay/.
11. Exodus 20:1.
12. Exodus Rabbah 5:9.
13. Cited in Martin Buber, *Tales of the Hasidim: Later Masters,* transl. Olga Marx, (New York: Schocken Books), pp. 300–302.
14. Deuteronomy 6:4–7. The entirety of this prayer, the Shema, consists

of Deuteronomy 6:4–7, Deuteronomy 11:13–21, and Numbers 15:37–41.

15. See James Kugel, *The God of Old: Inside the Lost World of the Bible* (New York: Free Press, 2003), chapter 5: "The Cry of the Victim."
16. Exodus 2:23–24.
17. Psalms 34:18–19.
18. Sefat Emet on Exodus 2:23.
19. Ohr Chadash 2:1.
20. Exodus 22:21–27; see also Job 34:28: "The cry of the poor comes before [God], who hears the cry of the needy."
21. Bill Moyers, "The Songs Are Free," February 6, 1991, https://billmoyers.com/content/songs-free/.
22. Shefa Gold, *The Magic of Hebrew Chant* (Woodstock, VT: Jewish Lights Publishing, 2013), pp. 7–8.
23. *Touch the Sound: A Sound Journey with Evelyn Glennie,* directed by Thomas Riedelsheimer (Munich: Filmquadrat, 2005).
24. Treasure, *How to Be Heard,* location 2000.
25. I Kings 19:11–12.
26. Song of Songs 5:2.
27. David Jaffe, *Changing the World From the Inside Out: A Jewish Approach to Personal and Social Change* (Boulder, CO: Trumpeter Books, 2016), pp. 32–33.
28. Rabbi Shalom Noah Barzovsky, *Netivot Shalom al HaTorah* (Jerusalem: Yeshivat Beit Avraham Slonim, 1982), on *parshat Yitro*.
29. Joey Weisenberg, *The Torah of Music* (New York: Hadar Press, 2017), pp. 27–28.
30. Rabbi Kalonymus Kalman Shapira, from Tzav veZiruz #36 and Hachsharat Avrekhim 9:3. Translation from Yitzhak Buxbaum, *Jewish Spiritual Practices* (Oxford, UK: Jason Aronson, 1990), adapted.

6. Rock of My Heart

1. Psalms 28:1, 31:2–4, 71:3.
2. II Samuel 22:1–3.
3. While not a direct biblical quote, these lyrics combine the metaphor of God as rock with the King James translation of Isaiah 32:2.
4. https://archive.culturalequity.org/node/61555

5. Patricia Adams Farmer, "The Numinosity of Rocks," Open Horizons, https://www.openhorizons.org/the-numinosity-of-rocks.html.

6. Isaiah 26:4.

7. "Honey from the Rock: The Contribution of God as Rock to an Ecological Hermeneutic," in *Exploring Ecological Hermeneutics,* ed. Norman C. Habel and Peter Trudinger (Atlanta: Society of Biblical Literature, 2008), p. 97.

8. Psalms 73:26.

9. Malbim on Psalm 73:26.

10. Nita Gilger, "Every Crevice a Story: The Boulder as Teacher," Open Horizons, https://www.openhorizons.org/every-crevice-a-story-the -boulder-as-teacher.html.

11. Genesis 28:18–19.

12. Exodus 24:4.

13. Joshua 4:2–22.

14. Joshua 4:21.

15. You can learn more about the memorial and read the full text of Alexander's poem at Renée Ater, "The Power of Remembrance: EJI National Memorial for Peace and Justice," April 27, 2018, https://www.reneeater .com/on-monuments-blog/2018/4/26/the-power-of-remembrance-1.

16. "Honey from the Rock," p. 102.

17. Deuteronomy 32:3–4.

18. Deuteronomy 32:15.

19. Deuteronomy 32:12–13, 18.

20. Exodus 17:5–6.

21. Isaiah 26:4.

22. You can see her introduction and the instructions at Jill S. Schneiderman, "Happy bEARTHday: Celebrate with 'A Body Scan Through Geologic Time,'" Lion's Roar, October 22, 2010, https://www .lionsroar.com/happy-bearthday-celebrate-with-a-body-scan-through -geologic-time/.

7. The God-Cloud

1. Exodus 13:21.

2. Exodus 14:19–20.

3. Exodus 14:24.

4. Psalms 105:39.

5. Nehemiah 9:19.

6. Exodus 40:38.

7. There is archaeological evidence in Israel and neighboring countries of ancient "fog (or dew) catchers"—stone structures that trapped water condensation from the air for farming. Perhaps the column of cloud represented just such a source of life-giving water for the authors of the Torah.

8. "What Are Clouds?," NASA, April 13, 2011, https://www.nasa.gov/audience/forstudents/5-8/features/nasa-knows/what-are-clouds-58.html.

9. Numbers 14:14.

10. Exodus 33:9, 11.

11. Exodus 24:15–16, 18.

12. Exodus 34:4–5.

13. Exodus 16:9–10.

14. Numbers 12:4–5.

15. Exodus 19:16, 20:15–18.

16. *Sefer Likutei MoHoRaN*, I, Section 115.

17. "Approaching the Thick Cloud: Working with Obstacles in our Spiritual Growth," in *Jewish Mysticism and the Spiritual Life: Classical Texts, Contemporary Reflections*, ed. Lawrence Fine, Eitan Fishbane, and Or N. Rose (Woodstock, VT: Jewish Lights Publishing, 2011).

18. *The Empty Chair: Finding Hope and Joy—Timeless Wisdom from a Hasidic Master, Rebbe Nachman of Breslov*, adapted by Moshe Mykoff and the Breslov Research Institute (Woodstock, VT: Jewish Lights Publishing, 1994), p. 14. For the context of this story, go to https://breslov.org/lookedatsky/.

19. From *Kitzur Shnei Luchot Habrit*, quoted in Michael Strassfeld, *A Book of Life: Embracing Judaism as a Spiritual Practice* (Woodstock VT: Jewish Lights Publishing, 2006), page 4, adapted.

8. Holy Fire

1. Joseph Bourke, "Encounter with God in the Old Testament," *Life of the Spirit* 15, no. 177 (March 1961): 400.

2. Deuteronomy 1:31–33.
3. Exodus 3:1–5.
4. Deuteronomy 4:24.
5. Exodus 3:6.
6. Deuteronomy 5:19–23.
7. Leviticus 10:1–2.
8. Exodus 32:9–10.
9. See Numbers 11:1, 16:35.
10. Psalms 79:4.
11. Nissim Amzallag, "Furnace Remelting as the Expression YHWH's Holiness: Evidence from the Meaning of Qanna' in the Divine Context," *Journal of Biblical Literature* 134, no. 2 (summer 2015): 233–252.
12. Ibid., 247.
13. For the entire exchange, see Exodus 3:7–4:17.
14. Exodus 22:21–22.
15. Ezekiel 36:5–7.
16. See Isaiah 9, 10.
17. "Police Violence, Race and Protest in America," *Economist,* June 4, 2020, https://www.economist.com/leaders/2020/06/04/police-violence-race-and-protest-in-america.
18. "Behind the Flames, a Burning Rage for Lost Lives," *Boston Globe,* May 30, 2020.
19. Audre Lorde, "The Transformation of Silence into Language and Action," in *Sister Outsider* (Berkeley, CA: Crossing Press, 1984).
20. Leviticus 6:5–6.
21. From the *Or HaMeir* in *Your Word Is Fire: The Hasidic Masters on Contemplative Prayer,* ed. and trans. Arthur Green and Barry W. Holtz (New York: Schocken Books, 1987), p. 51.
22. Sefat Emet on Tzav 3:23, in *The Language of Truth: The Torah Commentary of the Sefat Emet,* trans. and int. Arthur Green (Philadelphia: Jewish Publication Society, 1998).
23. Frederick Buechner, *Wishful Thinking: A Seeker's ABC* (New York: HarperCollins 1998), p. 119.
24. In the ancient Indian practice of yoga, candle meditation is called *trataka.* There is also a Jewish mystical practice of gazing at a candle

in order to come into awareness of God's presence. See Aryeh Kaplan, *Jewish Meditation: A Practical Guide* (New York: Schocken Books, 1985), pp. 69–72, for an explanation and instructions.

25. Quoted in *God in All Moments: Mystical and Practical Spiritual Wisdom from Hasidic Masters,* ed. and trans. Or Rose and Ebn D. Leader (Woodstock, VT: Jewish Lights Publishing), p. 77.

26. "Boston Hip-Hop Artists in This Moment," *Boston Globe,* July 26, 2020.

27. Alan Morinis, *Everyday Holiness* (Boston: Trumpeter, 2007), p. 59. Dr. Morinis attributes the "match and fuse" metaphor to his teacher, Rabbi Yechiel Yitzchok Perr.

28. Zelig Pliskin, *Anger: The Inner Teacher* (New York: Mesorah Publications, 1997).

29. See Leviticus 6:1–6.

9. Becoming

1. *Parable of the Sower* (New York: Four Walls Eight Windows Press, 1993), p. 22.

2. For an accessible introduction to Whitehead's philosophy, see C. Robert Mesle, *Process-Relational Philosophy: An Introduction to Alfred North Whitehead* (West Conshohocken, PA: Templeton Foundation Press, 2008).

3. Ibid., p. 85.

4. Exodus 3:11–14.

5. Cited in Santiago Sia, *God in Process Thought* (Dordrecht, Netherlands: Marinus Nijhoff Publishers, 1985), p. 39.

6. Deuteronomy 30:19.

7. Midrash Tehillim 90:13; see also Genesis Rabbah 3:7.

8. Octavia Butler, *Parable of the Talents* (New York: Seven Stories Press, 1998), p. 87.

9. With thanks to Cantor Sue for resharing this story with me with all of the details; you can learn more about her writing and teaching at cantorsue.com.

10. This quote derives from an interview about King with Marian Wright Edelman; see "Take the First Step in Faith. You Don't Have to See the Whole Staircase, Just Take the First Step," Quote Investigator, April

18, 2019, https://quoteinvestigator.com/2019/04/18/staircase/ for details.

11. Sharon Salzberg, *Faith: Trusting Your Own Deepest Experience* (New York: Riverhead Books, 2002), p. 81.

12. http://www.hilgart.org/1-living-in-radical-uncertainty.php, emphasis added.

13. adrienne maree brown, *Emergent Strategy: Shaping Change, Changing Worlds* (Chico, CA: AK Press, 2017), pp. 69–70, emphasis added.

14. From "God in Search of Man," quoted in Alan Morinis, *Everyday Holiness: The Path of Mussar* (Boston: Trumpeter, 2007), p. 238.

15. brown, *Emergent Strategy,* pp. 71–75.

16. In *Itturei Torah* (Tel Aviv: Yavneh Publishing House, 1996) on Exodus 3:14, volume 3, page 32.

17. Arthur Green, *Seek My Face, Speak My Name* (Woodstock, VT: Jewish Lights Publishing, 2003), p. 19.

18. *Kedushat Levi* on Rosh Hashanah.

19. Midrash Tanchuma, *Zot HaBrakhah* 7.

20. With profound gratitude to my colleague, Rabbi Jeremy Schwartz, for first introducing me to the idea that we can call God by the gerunds, the present-tense verb names found in our liturgy.

21. Estelle Frankel, *The Wisdom of Not Knowing: Discovering a Life of Wonder by Embracing Uncertainty* (Boulder, CO: Shambhala Publications, 2017), p. 53.

22. Ibid., p. 54.

23. Babylonian Talmud, Brachot 4a.

10. The Material World

1. II Samuel 6:2–7.

2. "What Is Electricity?," SparkFun, https://learn.sparkfun.com/tutorials/what-is-electricity/all.

3. Menachot 43b.

4. Genesis 3:9.

5. From "Christmas Sermon on Peace," 1967, in *A Testament of Hope: The Essential Writings and Speeches of Martin Luther King, Jr.*, ed. James M. Washington (San Francisco: Harper, 1986).

6. David Jaffe, *Changing the World From the Inside Out: A Jewish*

Approach to Personal and Social Change (Boulder, CO: Trumpeter Books, 2016), p. 87. The chapter "The Power of Choice" (pp. 82–99) delves more deeply into choice points and how they come up not just in our personal lives but also in the realm of organizational growth and the work of social change.

The End and the Beginning

1. Mishnah Brachot 4:2.